TWIST

How Fresh Perspectives
Build Breakthrough Brands

Laree —
Thank you for sharing
your gifts with the world.
Keep Twisting!

JULIE COTTINEAU
Founder of Brand School

TWIST

First published in 2016 by

Panoma Press Ltd
48 St Vincent Drive, St Albans, Herts, AL1 5SJ, UK
info@panomapress.com
www.panomapress.com

Book design and layout by Neil Coe.

Printed on acid-free paper from managed forests.

ISBN 978-1-784520-84-7

The right of Julie Cottineau to be identified as the author of this work has been asserted in accordance with sections 77 and 78 of the Copyright, Designs and Patents Act 1988.

A CIP catalogue record for this book is available from the British Library.

This book is available online and in bookstores.

TESTIMONIALS

"This book is a gift to small business owners, packed with information and strategies for potent branding, and full of obvious experience, wisdom and from-the-ground knowledge."

**- Sarah Hinawi, executive director,
Purpl Center for Learning and Social Innovation**

"This bold book encourages entrepreneurs and brand owners across all types of businesses to think outside the limits of their category and take risks, and gives them the tools to make them stand out from their competitors."

**- Laura Winston, attorney,
Kim Winston LLP**

"Julie's rich experience as the vice president of brand for Virgin has been brought to life in TWIST – a wakeup call and a road map for building brands that break through and get noticed."

**- Raul Leal, CEO
Virgin Hotels**

DEDICATION

This book is dedicated to the most inspiring people I know – Fred, Chloe and Sacha – you bring the TWIST that adds love and joy to my life every day.

And to my mother, Leona Curhan, who was my first editor and has always encouraged me to follow my dreams.

ACKNOWLEDGMENTS

Many people were instrumental in helping make this book a reality.

First of all, thank you to the Brand School students and BrandTwist clients who shared the journeys to their own TWISTS. They are mentioned by name in the book as we tell their stories.

Thank you to my draft readers whose comments helped reshape and refine the content: Randi Curhan, Courtney Glynn, Sarah Hinawi, Mike Mulligan, Eric Pickens, Heather Reid and Laura Winston. Special thanks to Jean Carucci for her comments and vital daily support at Brand School and Nola Kende Long for her perseverance and invaluable organizing, editing and cheerleading.

My friend and former colleague Gary Singer whose who/what/why/how framework I have embraced and TWISTED to become my own. I am grateful for your inspiration and friendship.

Thank you to Raul Leal and the gang at Virgin who taught me to "Screw It, Let's Do It."

Janice Spector, my dear friend and mentor, who helped me embark on a journey to France that changed my life.

To the Friday morning women's entrepreneur group at Purpl for your biweekly inspiration, wisdom and support.

The faculty at Brand School Online for generously sharing your expertise each semester.

Mindy Gibbins-Klein, Emma Herbert and the team at Panoma Press for your guidance and support.

Jamie Freitas, David Langton, and Alison Sheehy for helping with critical decisions when I was wavering.

Bob Plotkin, the uber talented photographer, who makes me shine in the cover photo and on my websites in all my purple outfits.

And to all my friends and family whose on-going support is invaluable and so appreciated.

"To teach is to learn twice over." ~ Joseph Joubert

CONTENTS

CHAPTER 1:
GREAT BRANDS ARE STORIES WITH A TWIST

Branding has become a buzzword and one of the most overused and least understood terms in marketing and business lexicon. There are many definitions of brand. Some that I often hear from participants in my workshops and classes include:

- How people ask for you: the name of your product or service.

- How people identify you: a logo, packaging and a website.

- How people perceive you: your image and identity.

- The experience people have with you: their emotional connections.

All of the above are true, but here's the definition of brand that I like the best for its power and simplicity. *A great brand is a story well told.*

This book will fully explore what I believe branding to be, how it is a constantly evolving and dynamic exercise, and how it is crucial to the success of your business. I will teach you how to build your own powerful brand story that stands out from the competition, helps you attract and retain profitable customers, and helps your business reach its full potential. Drawing on the lessons I've learned and the stories I've helped build during a

30-year career in the business of branding, I will provide tools and guidance to help you develop your own unique brand.

Let me start with my own brand story when 30 seconds at an airport led to a TWIST that changed my life.

The Birth Of The TWIST

During the winter of 2002 I was working as the executive director of consumer branding at Interbrand, a global branding agency. On a business trip to a client in Nebraska, I ran into the typical hiccups of flight travel from the New York metropolitan area: traffic, long lines at security, and countless departure gates leading to a maze of different airlines. Anticipating a less than fun-filled flight with mediocre airline food, a bland atmosphere, and the inevitable hurry up and wait pace of airline travel, I already felt defeated as I rushed toward my gate.

As I looked out the window to the tarmac, I was suddenly stopped by the image of a 747 airplane with McDonald's golden arches on the tail fin. Finally, here was something new and different! I envisioned what this McDonald's airline would be like. I imagined it would be good value with a flexible menu of ticket options and upgrades. It might allow me to "supersize" my experience to a seat with more legroom or special menu offerings. The interior of the plane would surely be brighter, more welcoming, and have attendants with a friendly service-oriented attitude. Maybe there would even be a fun "happy meal" type reward at the end of the trip. This McDonald's airline experience was dramatically more appealing to me than the plane I was about to board two gates down.

As it turns out, this airline was imaginary as it was the reflection of McDonald's yellow neon arches at the food court perfectly positioned onto a plane parked behind the window. While this McDonald's airline wasn't real, it led me to the very real practice of TWISTING brands in different categories to come up with new ideas. This "a-ha" moment became the inspiration for all of the work I was to do from that point forward in my corporate positions as well as my teaching positions, and then when I founded my own branding consultancy and branding school for entrepreneurs and small businesses. It is the reason I named my company BrandTwist.

The TWIST is the special sauce - it is looking outside of your category and finding inspiration in other successful brands. What does McDonald's have to do with airlines? Nothing. And that's the point. If you spend all of your time thinking about what other similar companies are doing, you will end up with a "me-too" product experience.

I have shared and applied this TWISTING approach to hundreds of student and client branding challenges over many years, helping unlock new perspectives and ideas that move brands forward in the marketplace. TWISTING is a no-fail technique that done within the right framework unleashes an astonishing number of high-quality, actionable ideas in a relatively short amount of time.

My TWISTING Background

In my own life, I've had a lot of personal and professional TWISTS that have reinforced my belief in the positive impact of TWISTING. I studied at the University of Pennsylvania Annenberg School of Communications to be a TV journalist. During a summer semester in London, I took the only open work/study spot that was available. It was in advertising, not journalism as I had hoped. I spent three months as an intern for a global advertising agency creating new product and marketing ideas for a leading chocolatier. I discovered I loved advertising and the fusion of creativity and strategy. My first life TWIST led me away from my journalism ambitions toward a new career path.

Upon graduation, I worked for Grey Global, an advertising agency, helping build powerhouse brands. I was happily ensconced in the New York City advertising scene when my life was TWISTED a second time after being transferred to the Grey Paris office, with little notice and no French language skills. Several wonderful years and a lovely French husband later, I was transferred back to the New York Grey Global office. I TWISTED again as another chance opportunity to become the executive director of consumer branding at Interbrand would lead me away from advertising and on a journey toward that fateful day at the airport.

After my McDonald's airline inspiration, I began infusing this concept of TWISTING into all of my branding work at Interbrand, which led to a record number of new ideas in each client session we held. The concept of TWISTING became so successful for each of our clients that I eventually caught the attention of executives at Virgin Management in NY who hired me as their vice president of brand.

Virgin was founded by the king of TWISTING Sir Richard Branson.

Richard was originally a record company executive in the 1970s with absolutely no experience running an airline. Bored with traditional airlines and the staid flying experiences they offered, he conceived of a more fun, "party in the sky" experience complete with a disco ball and a full-service cocktail bar in the cabin. With these TWISTED ideas and a mind to shake things up, Virgin Atlantic Airways was born. Since its origin, the Virgin brand has grown into a global conglomerate with core businesses in areas as diverse as travel, entertainment and lifestyle, financial services, healthcare, food and drink, media and telecommunications – even space ships!

It was a dream job to work at Virgin Management. My tenure involved working within many departments, businesses, and on a huge variety of branding projects. But one of the most important aspects of my time there was the opportunity to work with entrepreneurs from all categories. I was hooked on the idea of working with small businesses and entrepreneurs and this became a pivotal TWIST in my personal and professional narrative.

"Screw It, Let's Do It" Leads To BrandTwist And Brand School

Richard's motto "Screw It, Let's Do It" is known to those within the Virgin community and to any who follow his brands. With this mantra in mind, I left Virgin to start my own business BrandTwist with the goals of shaking the branding business up and teaching entrepreneurs to use their brands as actionable business tools while growing their businesses into profitable companies.

Before I founded my company, I first examined the gaps in the branding marketplace to ensure that I could offer something new and different. I found a huge underserved community of small business owners such as entrepreneurs, mom-and-pop businesses, solopreneurs, and non-profit organizations. Each of these business owners needed to stand out in the marketplace and to do so quickly with limited resources. They had passion, ideas, and sometimes employees, but limited understanding of branding and how their brand could serve them. I dedicated my company, BrandTwist, and my online Brand School by BrandTwist, to helping people understand, but most importantly TWIST, their brands to be focused and relevant in order to attract higher value customers, break out in crowded marketplaces and to impact their bottom lines.

What Is The TWIST?

There are two primary meanings of TWIST: 1) a *noun;* an unexpected change in a process or a departure from a usual pattern and 2) a *verb;* to weave together two separate entities to form a stronger single-strand. Brand TWISTING applies these definitions to the business world. Brand TWISTING is branding in action. That action involves looking out of your category at successful brands for inspiration and then applying those best practices by TWISTING them with your brand and business to create concrete ideas and approaches that help you stand out. It involves creating a unique brand story, identifying the tangible and intangible differences that you bring to your business, knowing what sets you apart from other companies that offer the same basic products and services, and how your personal experience and personality bring your brand and business to life.

Brand TWISTING Is Critical For Small Businesses And Entrepreneurs

Frequently I meet small business owners and entrepreneurs who are not sure they even need a brand, let alone one with a TWIST. I often get asked, "Most of my business is word of mouth, do I really need a brand?" "My business is just myself. No employees. People aren't brands, right?" and "I'm a business-to-business company, does branding even matter?"

My reply is always the same: branding matters for small businesses, entrepreneurs, non-profits, and personalities such as artists, actors and authors – perhaps even *more* than large corporations. Why? Because any business in a competitive marketplace, where stakes are high and budgets are low, needs to get its brand and its accompanying story across to potential customers quickly and with great impact. Your brand is a story of what makes your products and services unique. Getting that story right is one of the most important things you can do for the financial health of your business. And to craft the best story possible, you need to TWIST.

How Will A TWIST Help Different Businesses?

Entrepreneurs are typically rich with ideas and poor on resources. Brand TWISTING will help you focus and make the most of every precious dollar while getting other people on-board to help you bring your idea to market and spread the word.

Established businesses, both small and large, often face heavy competition or are weighed down by bureaucracy and committees. Brand TWISTING will help you create fresh ideas and stand out from your competition.

Non-profits are often fighting to secure donors and volunteers, with a small and under-budgeted staff. Brand TWISTING will help you connect emotionally with donors and get support for the critical work you do.

Business-to-business companies sometimes lose their excitement and uniqueness in an effort to appear serious and professional. Brand TWISTING will help you connect with business-to-business clients on a deeper, more profitable level.

Start TWISTING Now

Often I hear a small business owner say, "I'm not ready to work on my branding yet; I first have to get my business idea sorted out." This is incorrect logic and a possible financial mistake. Why? Defining the key elements of your brand story, in particular your target audience and the unique way you meet their needs, is central to the health of your business (even if you have been operating for some time). If you are just starting your business, it will help you create a name, logo, website and prototype product ideas. This, in turn, makes it easier for people to see and feel your vision.

Defining your unique TWIST will help you more quickly identify people (individuals, investors, agency partners) who can offer invaluable support in fast-tracking your success and makes your idea more tangible and legitimate. It helps others understand the opportunity so they can offer advice, support, and get on-board. Many entrepreneurs I meet have really interesting ideas, but they can't seem to express them in a succinct and powerful way to others.

I spent almost two years with the development team of Virgin Hotels presenting to potential investors. We spent time in these initial meetings talking about capital requirements, building costs, investment terms and returns, but the most captivating part of our meetings was when we talked about the brand TWIST for Virgin Hotels. We didn't have all of the details of the services and rooms nailed down but we had enough elements – a clear target, a point of differentiation, and key moments of magic throughout the hotel experience – to get investors on board and excited. This helped move Virgin Hotels from concept to reality, with its flagship hotel opening in Chicago in 2015.

Your Brand TWIST Should Influence Every Decision You Make

Brand building is not easy. Many people have great ideas, but what will make you a successful entrepreneur is your ability to bring your idea to life. Identifying your brand TWIST can help you say yes to the right opportunities, stay focused, and bring your brand and idea to market, but just as important it can also help you say no when necessary. A clear brand TWIST is also critical for internal alignment. Writing and sharing your TWIST within your company helps ensure everyone from the CEO to the receptionist is presenting a unified vision of the brand. Your employees should be able to answer the question "What does your company do?" highlighting your unique TWISTS. Using your brand as a filter for business decisions is smart business.

When I was the vice president of brand for Virgin Management, my job was to work with the business development team and review opportunities for Virgin to expand into new market segments, make recommendations, find or develop funding, and launch new ideas.

Our branding and business development team was small with a core group of five people. We often had difficulty agreeing on which opportunities to pursue and which to pass on because we all had a slightly different definition of what was "on-brand" for Virgin. While some of the team thought Virgin equaled travel, others thought it meant youth and rock and roll music. Despite our different definitions, there were some key fundamentals that defined the Virgin brand.

Once we focused on Virgin's core brand TWISTS of shaking things up, championing the consumer, and providing different and better customer service and experiences, we were able to have more productive conversations based on a common definition of the strengths of the Virgin brand. Ultimately, we created a brand-filtering tool that allowed us to assess new opportunities quickly so that we could move forward with those that were on-brand and pass on those off-brand ideas that would divert our valuable resources and dilute our clear brand story.

Build A Strong Brand TWIST That Has Tangible Value

Strong brands have tangible value. They will:

1. Minimize consideration of other brands.

2. Prompt requests for your brand by name.

3. Get recommended to friends and strangers.

4. Increase trial of new products and services.

5. Enable you to charge a premium.

6. Be forgiven when mistakes happen.

One of the strongest brands ever created is Apple, with its brand value estimated at $145 billion. [Source: Forbes.com] You don't need a branding study to prove Apple's value, just look at the hordes of people who line up on the street for each new upgrade, or set the blogosphere on fire when there is product news, or the unique fact that it never discounts its products.

How do you create a brand that has tangible value, is authentic and stands out? How do you TWIST? It starts with looking at your story from new angles. Cast aside the dos and don'ts, colors and imagery and so-called best practices of your competitors, and find a new way to attack old problems by using an out-of-category perspective. Stop thinking like a businessperson and think like a consumer. Think of brands that you love in all areas of your life and learn how to use these brands to inform and influence your own branding strategy and execution. I will show you how to TWIST up these lessons with your business to give new direction and life to your brand. I will give you actionable advice, tools and real examples from real Brand School students and BrandTwist clients that you can use to build your brand. This book is dedicated to helping you find and leverage your own brand TWIST to build a healthy and profitable business.

CHAPTER 2:
TWIST APART FROM YOUR COMPETITION

Take Off Your Brand Blinders

As a small business owner or entrepreneur, you are more than likely walking around with "brand blinders" on. This is when you spend so much time following the branding and marketing rules of your category that you end up completely blending in. Look at the marketing of your nearest competitors. Is there anything that you really admire or really stands out? Chances are no. In fact, if you printed out the home pages of five brands in your competitive set and crossed out all of the logos, would you be able to tell who is who? If you looked at all these printouts would most of the imagery look the same? Is there a predominant color that everyone is using? Are the key messages identical? If so, then you need to step away and take off your brand blinders.

Let me give you an example. Close your eyes and think about any bank you know. Think about their logo. What color is it? Chances are strong that it is predominately blue and red. (Citibank, Bank of America, HSBC and Chase all follow this rule.) Then imagine there was a section on the website talking about saving for retirement. Close your eyes again. What's the image you see? When I ask this question in my Brand School workshops, everyone immediately blurts out the same image: "Stylish couple in their 60s who are fit, dressed in white, and usually walking barefoot on a beach. They have short gray hair and piercing blue eyes that look off into the sunset with longing. They appear to have confidence in their financial future."

Try this again using websites for health coaches. There will probably be lots of logos with sunrays, waves, or overlapping concentric circles, plus women in yoga poses and rocks piled up on top of one another.

TWIST Away From The Pack

Why is fitting in a problem? As a business owner your potential customer is not just living in a world where your brand exists. As consumers we are overwhelmed with choices (it is estimated that we see 1,500-4,000 ads a day, but remember only 76), so standing out becomes critical. [Source: Belch & Belch: *Advertising and Promotion*]

Let's consider Starbucks, which comes up often on my students' best-loved brands list. Does it look and feel the same as other coffee shops? No, it doesn't because it has a unique living room-like atmosphere with comfy leather chairs, and the employees wear green aprons and look more like Italian baristas than typical fast-food servers. There is even a unique language spoken at Starbucks with a tall, venti, or grande replacing traditional sizes. Starbucks stands out because of its unique TWIST on the typical coffee experience; it has reinvented the definition of what a coffee brand should look and feel like. As a result, Starbucks is able to charge a substantial premium for its coffee over competitors even though blind taste tests have revealed that consumers prefer McDonald's coffee for taste. People are paying for the brand experience Starbucks provides regardless of the taste of the coffee. [Source: *Consumer Reports*, August 2009]

To highlight my point, when is the last time you said to a potential client or networking connection, "Let's meet at McDonald's and discuss this project"? You haven't because Howard Schultz, Starbucks' creator, created a different kind of coffee experience based on community not coffee. That is his TWIST.

Services, Not Just Products, Also Need A Strong TWIST

This sense of sameness is not just an issue for product branding, it's an issue for service companies as well. Often companies pitch with the same approaches and the same benefits, such as providing high quality, responsiveness and trustworthiness in their services or products. The words may be true but they have lost their meaning. Remember in the Peanuts comic strip all Charlie Brown heard was "wah, wah, wah, wah" when his teacher was speaking? In my Brand School class we often use this expression to describe undifferentiated brand promises and the effect they have on your clients' ears.

I experienced this on my first day as the vice president of brand at Virgin Management. After 20-plus years on the agency side making the pitch, this was my first time on the client side buying the services. We were looking for an agency to help us with branding for the Virgin Music Festival. We called in five talented firms on one day and heard one pitch after another. Although these were great firms that had come recommended by respected sources, they all sounded the same.

Each talked about their "proprietary process" (which was nearly the exact same steps in the exact same order and therefore not so proprietary). After a few hours of this "wah, wah, wah, wah" we were beginning to give up hope of an agency that could help us deliver a standout live music experience. Finally an agency came in with a TWIST. Instead of presenting the same credentials and processes, they focused on the music. They told us about their employees as people, their music tastes, what they liked about live events, and what they thought could be improved. They even showed photos of their creative team attending past Virgin Music Festivals (later called the Virgin Mobile FreeFest in the U.S.) to back up their claims. Their TWIST on presentation and personality broke through the static noise of the pitch day. They were hired, and it was the start of a long and productive relationship.

Connect To Your Audience With A TWIST

What did this agency do right? And what can your business learn from this? They put themselves in the heads of our consumers, which showed they would really help us brand effectively to our end-user. They shared some relevant, personal information that helped us see them as people we would like to get to know and work with.

I had a similar experience when visiting colleges with my daughter. After a while it is really hard to tell one school from another. They tell the same jokes: "Undecided? That's our most popular major." They emphasize the same benefits, and many even look the same with the same brand colors and logo styles (think blue or red academic shields) and often an undifferentiated style of "classic collegiate" architecture. If you did the website test where you blind the logos it would be truly hard to tell one school from the other. All of the sites feature smiling students, working in groups in the science lab, or having friendly but academic discussions out on the college green with blooming trees and ivy-covered buildings in the background.

After visiting nearly 20 schools, one college stood out for a very small, very inexpensive and highly impactful TWIST. We were in the middle of the hour-long tour and were in the cafeteria. We were listening to the same litany of dining benefits (choice, vegan, kosher, open 24 hours) that we heard everywhere else. However, the student tour guide broke from the expected script and encouraged us each to take a cookie or muffin as we passed the bakery case. This small gesture was really appreciated by the parents and students on the tour, it hardly cost anything, and it helped the tour guide make sure the hungry and tired parents and kids were able to continue to pay attention and absorb his message points.

Start Paying Attention To The TWISTS Around You

Become aware of brand experiences. Notice when you are having a positive brand experience, one where you are not just *buying* something you are *feeling* something. Make a note of the specific elements that are contributing to that feeling. It could be a small gesture like the cookie, an authentic story like the creative agency for the festival, or a fresh environment and unique language like Starbucks. Think of an idea that is inspired by these TWISTS and apply it directly to your brand to create something fresh and powerful. The trick to TWISTING is that it is an ongoing activity, not something you engage in every once in a while. You need to become a keen and constant observer of the larger brandscape. Always be thinking about your customer and what they need, and how you can apply lessons from other great brands to make your brand experience stronger and more unique.

Become An A+++ TWIST Master

In order to be an A+++ master of TWISTING, you need to follow the three As.

- Be AWARE of successful brand trends and practices all around you because your customer doesn't live in your category, they live in the larger brandscape. They are exposed to lots of messages, and only tune into the ones that break through. When you are in the mall or the supermarket, walking in town or the city, driving in the car listening to the radio, at the movies or watching TV – anywhere you go – start to notice brands that have interesting and unique messages. This can be distinctive packaging, TV ads, billboards, slogans, or brands that you hear your friends raving about or posting on social media. Carry a notebook around with you or record interesting brands with your cell phone camera. Becoming more brand aware – across all categories – is the first step.

- Then ANALYZE what is working. What human emotions and larger truths are being tapped into? What executional best practices do you see? What specifically is making you take notice? What is connecting with your heart, not just your head? Try to isolate specific strategies and techniques. Not just "that billboard was cool," but "it made me laugh, it was different from what everyone else is saying, it tapped into something I believe in or have been thinking about lately…."

- Lastly, APPLY these insights directly to your brand and act on them to create new ideas that you bring to market. Live in beta, that is, don't wait for an idea to be perfect, as perfection can be the enemy of progress. Get it to a point where it is good enough, then try it out – see what's working and what's not and then keep refining.

A Small Company Can Offer A Big TWIST

As a small business or non-profit, your best competitive advantage is standing out. What good is spending even one precious marketing dollar on an ad or a website if it's not going to break through? Your unique brand story is what customers want to hear. If they have made the decision to even consider smaller brands, they are eschewing the anonymity of big brands and are looking for a more personal connection.

Authenticity and personal connection have always been a competitive advantage for small businesses, but now it seems more so than ever. We are in the midst of the age of the entrepreneur, and perhaps this is in part a reaction to some of the mistakes and failures of some of the larger global brands (Enron, Lehman Brothers, BP). Or maybe it's because the global economy and politics feel a bit overwhelming and out of control. Regardless of why small businesses are resurgent, stop trying to pretend you are bigger than you are, with more offices and employees, and celebrate the fact that you offer deep connections and localized expertise.

> Linda, a Brand School student, has a family-owned insurance agency that celebrates its roots in the community. This includes a unique TWIST of sending out email advisories during bad weather with very localized updates on specific road closings and streets to avoid. This is something the larger companies could never do. And Linda's customers are grateful. It's one thing for an insurance agency to talk about its auto insurance policies, it's another for it to actually keep you safe on the road.

What makes your approach different? What is there specifically in your background that makes you better qualified than the next "quality" provider to provide an extra edge to your clients? Let your authenticity and humanity shine through your brand.

How can you do this? There are several approaches and here are a few examples.

Share Your Founder's TWIST

A great TWISTING strategy is to share the origin of how you came to create your brand. How did you first get the idea? What influences in your childhood or working past led you to this point today? Remember, this is a story that is more of a memoir than a biography. Craft it by leaving out points that are confusing or don't help to paint a clear picture of your path and TWIST.

> Barbara, a dentist, decided to go into dentistry after her father (a working class, first-generation immigrant) had spent all of his savings on a set of partials that were poorly made, which led to gum disease and the loss of his teeth. She carried those partials in her pocket all through dental school as a powerful reminder of why she wanted to help people so they wouldn't have to suffer like her dad. This is a beautiful TWIST with a very memorable image and she uses it to connect with her ideal target – people who feel their smiles are fundamentally linked to their life stories.

In my own case, my passion for branding began when I was eight years old. I had a pretty nice childhood in Marblehead, Massachusetts, in the early 70s. While I was a happy little girl, one thing was missing. I desperately wanted a pet: a dog, cat, hamster, something fuzzy to call my own. Unfortunately, my older brother was allergic to pet fur, so an animal was out of the question. Being eight, I went into our backyard garden, got a rock, put it in an empty Cool Whip container with a few blades of grass for nourishment, poked a few holes in the lid for it to breathe and ... voilà, instant pet rock. My parents looked at me kind of funny, but they were glad the "pet crisis" was over. They wouldn't realize I was a branding genius until a few years later.

In 1975, Gary Dahl, an advertising executive from Los Gatos, California, was sitting in a bar listening to friends complain about their pets and how they needed to be constantly walked and fed. He got the idea of creating the perfect no-maintenance pet. This led to the idea of selling Pet Rocks to people, complete with instructions. The instruction book was the real product, which was full of gags and puns. The fad was short-lived, but that was enough to make Dahl a millionaire.

He "stole" my idea. Of course, I was still a child and I didn't have the same wherewithal and resources as Gary to bring this idea to market. But I think it's an important story and one that I often tell when speaking to groups of aspiring entrepreneurs and even senior marketing and branding executives. My story has several important messages about branding and the importance of TWISTING. It has also become a key touch point in my own personal branding story.

On the surface, Gary and I have nothing in common: we are different ages, have different occupations and live in different parts of the country. But there are actually a lot of similarities to our stories:

- We were both trying to solve a consumer problem (mine was for a non-allergenic pet, his was for a low-maintenance one).

- We both TWISTED to think of a unique solution to an old problem. Rather than work within the traditional pet category to come up with our solutions, we looked elsewhere – to a rock.

The big difference between us was that my idea stayed within my immediate family and Gary managed to package and market his idea and share it with the world. Over time I came to recognize the importance of getting things out into the marketplace (versus waiting for everything to be perfect) and this bias toward action has become part of what drives me as a brand consultant and has become part of my personal TWIST.

Step Away To See Your Own TWIST More Clearly

Sometimes your TWIST is something that is so fundamental to your personality you actually overlook it. This is why it's a good idea to write your brand story and then have someone else review it. Often other people have the required distance to see important elements that you are overlooking or that you might be omitting because it feels like you are bragging. But you need to be passionate about your own brand TWIST – if not, how do you expect others to get excited about it?

> Liz, a graphic and web designer, is an avid amateur trapeze artist. Every waking moment that she is not spending creating websites and logos for clients is spent flying through the air – trying to master catching the bar from her partner and completing some aerial trick. Even though she is often bruised and bloodied from her trapeze practice, she can't get enough of it. Through her work at Brand School she realized that her love of acrobatics wasn't just a side hobby. It revealed something fundamental about her personality that was, in fact, very relevant to her design business. It is all about trust. Being able to let go of the trapeze bar and reach blindly for the hands of the other trapezist about to catch you is a proof point of a whole new height of relationship commitment. She began to infuse her branding with her love of trapeze. She rebranded her design services as "big top services," using an elegant circus visual design motif, and began deliberately talking about her hobby – presenting it as a "combination of fearlessness, honesty and creativity that you won't find anywhere else."

> Most importantly, she related this philosophy directly back to her approach to working with clients to create impactful designs. This trapeze TWIST is now infused throughout her rebranded website and really makes her stand out. By embracing and owning her TWIST she is able to present herself and her business as fearless, unique, creative, flexible and a devoted partner.

TWIST For A Name That Stands Out

The name of your company, product or service is your declaration of what you stand for. But too often small businesses gravitate towards "me-too" names with no personality or TWIST.

Focusing on a unique brand TWIST for a company name versus following the category norms is why Apple is a more distinctive name than Microsoft, Uber stands out versus Dial-a-Car, and Starbucks breaks through in a category of Dunkin' Donuts-sounding brands.

A name alone can't make or break a brand, but it does help to start a positive conversation with prospective customers by helping them understand quickly what you are about, what's different about you, and how you can help them. Just as you don't want your website and logo to look like all of your competition, you don't want your name to sound the same either.

Ryan and Rick are a dynamic duo with their own digital marketing and design firm. While they are very good at creating brand names, logos and websites for clients, they were stuck about what to do for their own brand. Ryan and Rick hated their company name and were embarrassed by their uninspired website. Their business name featured the concept of "creating a buzz" and it was chosen when the business launched "just to get something out there." They soon realized that it wasn't at all unique and didn't have a TWIST since many marketing companies, PR firms, digital companies and advertising agencies are all talking about buzz. In fact, it is such an overused term it no longer has any cachet or buzz factor. The name also didn't reflect their personalities, which are more fun and quirkier than the tired name would lead you to expect. So having a "me-too" name with no TWIST was not ideal for a talented company trying to convince other small businesses that they had what it takes to bring their brand to life in a unique and creative way.

This pair couldn't agree on a new name, and couldn't move forward with updating their brand. Then they enrolled in Brand School, took a step back and first defined their TWIST – what was really special about them. They spent time delving into their personalities, skill sets and how they were different from the multitude of other local digital design firms. Finally, they agreed that it was their ability to integrate all aspects of a client's marketing (logo, digital, traditional) and make these elements "play nice together" and they discovered the foundation of their TWIST. Once they landed on this brand

> idea they quickly came up with a new name, logo and design system that they were both excited about. They redid all of their own marketing materials in just two weeks!

Authentic TWISTS Create Connections To Your Target

Use your flaws to draw others in, to help them see themselves in your brand and want to be closer to it. One of my most popular Facebook posts was loosely related to branding but had a personal TWIST, which I believe drove its popularity. I recounted the story of how my twelve-year-old son complimented me on my new Nike running shoes (which was a *big* deal coming from a kid who, like many boys his age, was obsessed with sneakers). I was enjoying the moment, proud of my new "kicks" and the cool mom points I had scored when in the next breath he said, "Too bad you ruined your look by wearing them with your Adidas tennis socks." I posted this anecdote along with the summary line: "I guess this was one TWIST that didn't work." I got lots of likes and comments and it reminded me that it's important to show some vulnerability. I don't always have to be the branding expert sharing my insights; sometimes I can just be the mom trying to get a little admiration from my kids. This authenticity is an important part of my brand and something my target relates to.

> Tim runs an aquarium supply company and has an impressive list of professional credentials including a Ph.D. in ecology, evolution and marine biology. The "about me" section of his

website was a laundry list of academic degrees, published articles, industry titles and honors, but it practically required a Ph.D. to read and understand it. The problem? His ideal target included regular "Joe" aquarium enthusiasts who are looking for support in keeping their aquariums healthy and vibrant. Through the work Tim did in Brand School, he transitioned his brand idea from "science-based solutions" to "success at any level." He deliberately presents a less intimidating, more welcoming user experience where buyers feel more at ease to interact with the brand and ask more questions, in order to ensure that they are buying the right aquarium products for their specific needs. In the context of this revamped and more approachable brand communications, the old "about me" narrative really didn't fit.

The solution? Trimming his story down to the most essential credentials and then adding a more human TWIST. His revised story starts with this line: "I got my first aquarium at age six after killing two goldfish I had won at a school fair. Responding to the pleas of help from my mom, my uncle brought over an extra tank from his dentist office and showed me the basics. I still have that aquarium!" Do you see the difference this personal and authentic TWIST adds? It makes his brand more approachable, more relatable, and more likely to attract the amateur aquarium enthusiast who might be turned off by a brand that seems too scientific and overly authoritative.

You don't have to be a solopreneur to share personal elements. If you work for a small or medium-sized business, you can still be authentic. Do this by bringing the founder's story to life in a more personal way or celebrate the unique personalities of the current employees.

One of my favorite TWISTS is from Innocent – a very popular fresh smoothie brand in the U.K. This is the engaging story about the origin of the company that they tell on their website: "We started Innocent in 1999 after selling our smoothies at a music festival. We put up a big sign asking people if they thought we should give up our jobs to make smoothies, and put a bin saying YES and a bin saying NO in front of the stall. Then we got people to vote with their empties. At the end of the weekend, the YES bin was full, so we resigned from our jobs the next day and got cracking."

This approachable and self-deprecating tone of voice is consistent throughout their brand communications. In fact, another interesting TWIST is that they change their packaging labels quite frequently. Often they mix up the copy on the ingredients. One such label listed the ingredients as: "2½ pressed apples, 6 crushed strawberries, ½ mashed banana, a dash of freshly squeezed orange juice, and a few small pebbles*". There was an asterisk next to the pebbles and a comment further down at the very bottom of the label stating: "*we lied about the pebbles." This may be a small TWIST, but it's part of an overall approach and quirkiness that keeps customers coming back for more of Innocent. They have created a legion of loyal fans and have become a successful powerhouse in the drinks industry.

Express Your TWIST Consistently

You may get bored telling your story, but while it's repetitive to you, it's new each time for each new listener. Often people need to hear your story multiple times for it to register. And storytelling can be visual as well as verbal. A key element of my own brand story is the color purple. When I created BrandTwist and Brand School, I deliberately chose this color because it helps me stand out from the corporate branding agencies that use more conservative colors (grey, light yellow, red). I wanted to signal from the start (here's my TWIST) that I was going to bring my passion and personality to the table, and in turn, this was going to help my clients and students find and embrace their own unique TWISTS. So rather than just use purple on my website and business cards, I decided to embrace it in my wardrobe. I do a lot of presenting in front of live groups and in tele-classes as part of Brand School, so I decided that when I appear as an ambassador of my brand, I will always wear purple.

I hadn't realized how important this color had become to my brand TWIST until one summer evening during an appearance as the keynote speaker for a presentation on branding. Prior to the presentation, I was mingling with attendees. One woman, who I had not previously met in person, came running up to me to introduce herself. She excitedly shook my hand and breathlessly explained to me that she was a big fan of my work and of BrandTwist on Facebook. Then the conversation came to an abrupt halt. She took one look at my open-toed sandals and my red toenail polish and her face dropped. She said to me: "You know, you really should have purple polish on your toes." I had to admit that she was right. If purple was part of my TWIST, I should embrace it – from head to toe. And now I do.

Find The Right TWISTING Partners

Once you've found your unique TWIST, how do you bring it to life? This is where the right design or marketing partner can really make a difference. One of the biggest mistakes I see business owners make is hiring someone to do their website primarily because they have previous experience in their category. Look instead for a partner whose designs connect to their targets and break through. Ask them specifically how they would bring their own TWIST to your brand. How would they approach branding your law firm if you were a vodka or fashion brand? Include in your brief to the designers a list of brands outside of your category that you admire, and most importantly, why. These inspirational brands can be chosen using many factors. It could be a visual style or color that stands out, the way the brand seems to understand its consumers, extra features, or even the tone of voice the brand uses. The important thing is to delve into why you think it's effective, how it is meeting a similar need that your target has, and how it can inspire your unique brand solutions. Then discuss how you can leverage these TWISTS for your own brand.

Not long ago I was contacted by a financial services technology company in Boston that was disappointed with its current branding. They were looking for a resource to help them create a new brand position and fresh look and feel that would really break through in their cluttered category. They lamented that their business and all of their competitors looked and sounded alike. They were convinced that their technology-enabled cost management systems were truly better and different from the rest of the market, but they were at a loss as to how to bring this distinctiveness to life.

This sounded like a challenge perfect for me, and I told the marketing director over the phone about my experience in helping a wide range of clients stand out by using my specific TWISTING philosophy of looking outside the category for best practices and inspiration. She was really excited about this approach and wanted to double check with her boss prior to setting up a meeting. Unfortunately, her boss wanted a detailed account of my specific experience and credentials in the financial service industry, which was counter to the approach I had proposed. He wanted reassurance before hiring me that I was well-versed in the very category that he found mediocre and uninspired. In the end, I wished them well and declined the project.

CHAPTER 3:
DON'T MARKET UNTIL YOU DEFINE YOUR TWIST

Often I get asked the difference between branding and marketing. My response is that branding is your fundamental promise of whom you serve, how you make them feel and what's different about how you deliver. Marketing is how you get this message out there once you have defined it.

You will save time, money and energy by creating a well-defined brand before you hire anyone to do your marketing, even if you are doing all the marketing yourself.

Many small businesses come to me lamenting that they just can't find a quality resource to help them with their branding. Often they've been through as many as two or three web designers or marketing agencies and they still haven't gotten what they wanted. Here's my response: it's not the designer or the agency that is the problem, it's you. You have not done the fundamental work of defining your brand and you are providing them with very vague, undifferentiated messages with no TWIST and then waiting to be wowed.

Because branding is so fundamental to your business, finding your brand TWIST is crucial to creating a brand that breaks through and creating a strong brand is about asking questions.

Develop Your TWIST By Answering These Four Key Questions

Answering these four fundamental questions about your brand will become the basis of a powerful TWIST, which will then drive your marketing. The questions are deceptively easy to ask, but take hard work, a thorough exploration, and dedicated time and effort to answer.

THE FOUR KEY QUESTIONS

1.WHO? are the most profitable targets for the brand?

TWIST to zero in on specific emotional triggers

2.WHAT? will compel them to choose you and stay loyal?

TWIST to create a more distinctive brand promise

3.WHY? should these high-priority targets believe?

Add your personal TWIST for a stronger story

4.HOW? is the brand felt in every touch point?

TWIST with brands you admire for fresh ideas

BRAND**TWIST**™

1. WHO are the most profitable targets for the brand?

TWIST to zero in on specific emotional triggers

If you don't have a clear idea of "who" you want to serve with your brand, it doesn't matter how many mailing lists you purchase. This is the first, and probably, the most important question you need to grapple with. And it's hard. Because you may be saying to yourself: "I want everyone to feel welcome to buy my products or services. I don't want to leave anyone out or turn anyone away." This can be a mistake because when you market to everyone you risk connecting with no one. And when you do figure out exactly who your ideal target is, it's so much easier and less costly to find them because you then know where they hang out, who influences them, and what blogs and magazines they read.

2. WHAT will compel them to choose you and stay loyal?

TWIST to create a more distinctive brand promise

The question of "what" is about your core brand promise. It's the connection you make that is deep and lasting, the one that touches people's hearts, not just their heads. At Brand School, we call this brand promise the brand idea. Your brand idea is what you are offering to your target that makes them choose and stay loyal to you. It transcends any one product or service that you offer. It should connect with both the rational and emotional needs of your customer.

Your brand idea should influence every single decision you make for your business. Big decisions such as the products and services you offer, who you hire and partner with, what you charge, to seemingly smaller decisions like how you dress, how you decorate your office, what kind of holiday gift you send clients, to how you answer the phone, all come into play.

YOUR BRAND TWIST
SHOULD DRIVE EVERY DECISION

BRAND**TWIST**˙

A strong brand idea is especially important for small businesses and non-profits that may be resource-constrained because it helps simplify all of the business and marketing decisions you have to make. You can make these decisions faster and with more confidence because all roads lead to your brand idea and all your business-building efforts should be moving toward a unified impression (or story) for your target.

Your core brand idea should stay consistent over time, but how you bring it to life – your products and services and marketing campaigns – can and should be refreshed.

Your brand idea is one of the most fundamental areas of your brand story; a unique TWIST is imperative to stand out. Everyone can promise to help people get things done, but it's how you make them feel, what they will be able to accomplish with their lives when interacting with your brand that makes all the difference.

GREAT BRANDS AIM HIGHER

Think of strong brands that you admire and that stand out. Chances are that they are all participating in "top of the pyramid" branding. Nike's top of the pyramid promise is achievement ("Just Do It"), while many of its competitors spend their time at the bottom of the pyramid talking about fabrics, materials and cushioned soles that help you run faster.

I would define Apple's top of the pyramid promise as "imagination", while many other technology companies live at the bottom talking about storage, speed and functionality that is immediately outdated. Apple is promising us a vision of the world where with the swipe of a finger anything is possible. The problem with branding bottom of the pyramid functions such as features and price is that it leaves your brand vulnerable for a competitor to offer more and better. When you brand at the top of the pyramid, you create a stronger connection with your customer that is harder for someone else to usurp.

A strong brand idea is essential to stand out, no matter what your category. It's true for servers (IBM's "Solutions for a Smarter Planet") to sports drinks (Redbull's "Gives You Wings"). A brand idea is not necessarily a tagline, but a short, powerful encapsulation of what your brand stands for (which is often the basis of your tagline).

How do you create a powerful and differentiated brand idea? It goes back to the "who." First you need to get to know your ideal customer really, really well. Delve into their hopes, dreams and fears, what keeps them up at night and what do they really want out of life? These insights should be connected to your category but also go beyond that. You are looking for the specific TWIST that will make your target real. Once you have really explored your "who," then you begin to create the "what," by moving on to a benefit pyramid. You start at the bottom of the pyramid with what you offer and then you begin to transition to what this allows them to do, then feel, then ultimately to be.

The biggest challenge with creating a powerful brand idea is making sure it's distinctive, that it has your unique TWIST. Often on their first attempts, my students come up with very generic emotional benefits. These might include things like confidence, peace of mind, trust, and empowerment. What's the problem with these? We've heard them so many times in so many different categories that they've lost their meaning. Everyone from Oprah to the dry-cleaner is promising to help you feel "more empowered." To have a really strong brand in today's oversaturated markets, you have to dig deeper.

Strong brand ideas meet four key criteria. They are: 1) relevant to your target; 2) unique; 3) inspirational; 4) supportable.

Here are some examples of brand ideas from Brand School students and how they evolved through TWISTING so you can see the impact of being more specific and unique.

Insurance Agency:

From: "We Treat You Like Family"

To: "We Help You GET Insurance"

Eurythmy Teacher: (a form of movement used therapeutically)

From: "Eurythmy For Adults"

To: "Create a Connected Life"

Small Business Consultant:

From: "An Affordable Way To Create Business Plans"

To: "Drive Your Business Dreams Forward"

Video Production Studio:

From: "Video Marketing Solutions For Any Sized Business"

To: "Visualize Your Success With Video"

Creating a strong, differentiated brand idea is the single most important investment you will make in your business, and it will pay off. Having clarity on your brand will help you raise your prices and increase your negotiation leverage. Because when you are clearer on your ideal target and what you are really offering them (i.e., Starbucks = community not just coffee) then you will have more confidence in your value and only work with or sell to people who also value what you are offering and are willing to pay you what you are worth.

> Benan sells jewelry handcrafted from stones that are chosen with her sister and business partner who lives in Turkey. Through the target persona exercise, she realized that she isn't really selling jewelry. She is selling the ability for her customers to own a unique piece with a unique story to each stone, and in turn to express her own story. She created a new tagline for her business: "Centuries of Stories. Tell Yours." Benan also began creating mini brand stories for each of the pieces of jewelry – giving them specific names and talking about the origin of the style and the relevance in Turkish culture. The result? This shift from selling jewelry to selling stories allowed her to adjust her prices to where they deserved to be, given the time, love and craftsmanship that went into each piece. The customers are happy to pay the higher prices because the intrinsic value of what they are buying for themselves, and for gifts, is much clearer and stronger.

3. WHY should these high-priority targets believe?

Add your personal TWIST for a stronger story

The third important question that your brand needs to answer is "why." Why should people believe your promise? Why should they choose your brand among so many others to help them achieve their goals? As a small business owner you can really bring your unique TWIST to how you support your promise. Think of your brand idea as the overarching roof of your brand, the "why" is brought to life in brand pillars that support this roof. These pillars, which are discussed below, are the ways in which you consistently deliver your promise and the reason why your targets will believe you. These pillars reflect your brand values and the way you approach everything you do for your brand. They are bigger than any one piece of communication or program.

Can you answer the question "Why should my high-priority target choose my brand?" in a powerful and succinct way? This may seem like a fairly simple question to answer, but it's not. This is because we tend to fall back on pillars that have lost their meaning and don't stand out (i.e., high-quality, 25 years' experience, trustworthy) and partly because we don't like to promote ourselves. This is particularly true of women entrepreneurs. Many women feel that providing strong reasons why you should choose them is somehow bragging or unseemly. But you need to think about promoting your brand as "serving, not selling." When you talk about your brand with passion, conviction and a focus on how you can help people accomplish or feel something, then you are not selling, you are branding.

How do you create these unique brand pillars? We believe in the power of the three-point argument so you can remember them in your elevator pitches and your potential customers can also take them in. We call them the 3Ps. You will notice that each of these has a unique TWIST to make the pillar as strong and sturdy as possible.

Pillar #1: What do you bring *personally* to the table that is unique to your background and helps deliver the brand idea? What is your personal TWIST?

Pillar #2: What is your unique *point of view* on the category? This is often a reaction to what's missing from the way things are currently. What is your category TWIST?

Pillar #3: How does your unique *process/product* support the brand idea? What is your operational TWIST?

> Sara, who has a coaching business helping single moms feel in control and stop second-guessing their parenting decisions, developed her 3Ps this way. Her brand idea is: "Create priorities and plans for a kickass life." This is supported by three strong pillars that help her target understand "why" she is the right resource to trust with this important area of their lives.
>
> *Inspirational:* (*personal*) "*I have single mommed a child at every age and achieved some big personal goals. I will save you time and energy because I know what works and what doesn't.*"
>
> *Intuitive:* (*point of view*) "*I help single moms develop and trust their intuition so they can feel confident in their decision-making and begin to craft their dreams, goals and desires.*"
>
> *Implementable:* (*process*) "*Single momming is big and complex but I make the complex simple and develop a process that is understandable, implementable and easy to maintain so you can incorporate it into your life.*"

BRAND FRAMEWORK

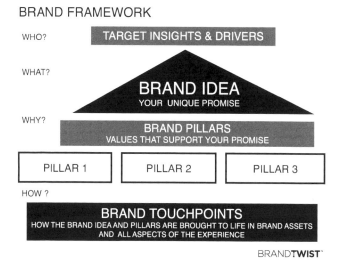

BRAND**TWIST**™

4. HOW is the brand felt in every touch point?

TWIST with brands you admire for fresh ideas

"How" is the last of the four key questions and it's where the marketing, social media and other activities finally come in. A brand promise and pillars are great on paper, but for them to have impact they must be felt in every interaction with your customer. It is really important to find your unique TWIST, and really fun to observe and learn from other brands.

Again, think about brands you love and their unique TWISTS. It could be as small as the message under the caps for Snapple, or the large and unique Genius Bar in all of the Apple stores. Find your own path, create your own TWISTS and even the smallest gestures will get you remembered and help you connect with your target.

To add some clarity, let your brand framework guide both your marketing and social media marketing activities. Think about who your target audience is. What are their social media habits? What channels do they favor? Are they even on Pinterest or Twitter? How does social media support your brand idea and pillars? For example, if you are promising community or transparency as part of your brand then using social media is probably pretty important. But make sure you use it strategically. Look again to brands that you admire for their approach and actions in social media. What are they doing? How does it make you feel? Then TWIST these insights into your own brand.

Alex, who is in the test prep business, took his inspiration from ESPN when creating a strategic social media plan. He was inspired by how ESPN uses different hash tags and custom twitter accounts based on shows or events: #ESPNCareers, #ESPNFirstTake and #ESPNNFL. He admired how the breadth of ESPN's online presence allows them to be viewed through a high number of searches, both for people and events, and further establishes their brand idea as the "worldwide leader in sports." He also liked how the speed and ease of use is particularly appealing to the tech-savvy younger generation, which both ESPN and his test prep company targets.

Alex's TWISTED idea was to set up specific hashtags for individual subjects (i.e., #calculus or #biology that included the company prefix) so that students could tag questions with this hashtag, and then he could have tutors set up to respond to those tweets at various intervals.

> This is an innovative TWIST that came from looking outside of the crowded category of tutoring and test prep to an inspirational brand like ESPN that also targets teens, but in a very different context.

Your brand is the promise that walks into the room ahead of you and sticks around long after you've gone. It's crucial to your business. In this internet era, your website is your business card. Even if you get most of your business from personal referrals, people are still going to check out your website. It's going to form a first impression and then be a source for continued reinforcement that your target has made the right choice. But before you begin any work on creating or updating your website, save yourself time and money by making sure your brand framework of who/what/why is clear and has a compelling TWIST.

CHAPTER 4:
STOP TARGETING EVERYONE, TWIST WITH TRIGGERS

One of the biggest branding mistakes I see small businesses make is that they target everyone. They have broad and generic advertising headlines and website copy that say things like:

"Are you trying to lose weight?"

"Does your business need help with accounting?"

"Do you want to find that special someone?"

"Do you wish you had healthier skin?"

"Do you need quality legal advice?"

"Are you looking for a full service marketing agency?"

While many people may nod their head yes to these descriptions, chances are very few will actually pick up the phone or click on a link to find out more. This is because when your brand stays at this very general level, it is hard for the target to see that you are really speaking to them, and feel connected and compelled enough to take action. They may like your Facebook page, but your relationship will probably stop there. Ask yourself, do you want a lot of friends and followers on Facebook or do you want actual customers?

Often I hear entrepreneurs tell me they don't want to alienate anyone or turn them away if they get too specific in their target customer. But the irony is that this is exactly what you are doing by targeting too broadly. People need to recognize themselves in your brand and really picture themselves benefiting from what you have to offer. In order to do this, you need to pick one ideal target and delve deep into what that target wants, needs and values so you can speak to these needs and connect with them.

Emotional TWISTS Drive Customer Connections

Successful brands don't go after broad demographic targets; they look for emotional triggers and insights that identify the customers with the highest potential. Then they leverage these triggers to attract them and convert them to rabid fans.

For example, the cosmetics category has hundreds of brands that are able to successfully co-exist in this arena. They all offer the same basic products: cleanser, moisturizer, toner, blush, eye shadow, and more. What's the main difference among all of these brands? They aren't all chasing the same group of women. The market is segmented by personality, values, attitudes, and interest – often called psychographic profiling. A woman who chooses Clinique, for example, is most likely looking for an approach to beauty that has a scientific side where the products are researched and formulated to be gentle. Women who buy their products from Lancôme are trying to get a piece of the French beauty ideal. Those who are taking care of their skin with Oil of Olay products available at mass market retailers instead of department stores feel smart knowing that they can buy excellent products without paying more for department store brands.

These differences in consumer insights enable many brands to co-exist in different categories. Take the hotel category, for example. There are literally thousands of choices in major cities where a business traveler could get a clean room and a comfortable bed. But these are just functional needs. What are the emotional needs? Traditional hotels like the Hilton and Sheraton believe that their customers are looking for consistency with no surprises. Customers want to know that they can expect the same thing in every city: a consistent level of amenities and service. Whereas travelers that stay at a W are looking for more action. They want to feel a part of the city's vibe they are visiting. And DoubleTree by Hilton gives out approximately 77,000 chocolate chip cookies each day adding up to more than 28 million cookies annually, which is part of their TWIST to attract those who want to feel welcome and like they are home.

Have you ever had the experience of picking up your favorite magazine and page after page is filled with articles about things you were "just thinking about"? That's because the editors have identified and understood your profile (and others like you) as their ideal reader, and curated the content with you in mind. This would not be the case if you picked up another magazine that might be for a person of your same age group, but with completely different interests.

Narrow targeting does not mean that only those people will be attracted to your brand. If you pick an aspirational target then you will attract your core target as well as people who admire or want to be like them. Apple has created the model of whom they are going after: a 20-something, hip, musically-inclined digital native just like the actor Justin Long who was cast as their brand ambassador in Apple vs. PC advertising. In actuality, Apple has users from age five to eighty-five, even though they are not directly targeting them in their branding and marketing. They are designing and branding products aimed at someone in a pretty narrow sweet spot. This 20-something digital native, in the area of technology mastery, is who we all want to be.

Microsoft, on the other hand, seems to focus on the technology and appears to be targeting anyone who has a specific functional need. They make great products, but don't tend to inspire the same kind of awe and loyalty as Apple, where people sleep out on the sidewalk for days waiting for the newest iPhone release.

Another example of an extreme, if not aspirational, target is the brand Poo-Pourri. Poo-Pourri is a line of essential oils that are specifically and unabashedly for toilet odors. This is a topic that many people are too embarrassed to acknowledge and talk about. Rather than dance around the issue, Poo-Pourri addresses it head on by featuring a very prim and proper British spokesperson in its ads. She is dressed for a cocktail party in a very elegant bright blue dress with pearls, a crinoline, and perfectly coiffed hair.

Poo-Pourri cleverly goes to the extreme by showing a target who is the last person we would expect to see *on* the toilet talking about the fact that "everyone poops" and how the odor barrier created by their product locks the offending scents in the bowl. Is Poo-Pourri targeting too narrow and only attracting the kind of woman portrayed in its ads? Of course not. It actually sells products for men, women, kids and even pets. But by focusing on this extreme target, the company is making the topic more accessible to everyone. It's a brilliant piece of targeting and no doubt contributes to the fact that the product, which was created and introduced by entrepreneur

Suzy Batiz in 2007, racked up $1 million in sales its first year. It is now generating over $15 million in sales per year.

[Source: imediaconnection.com]

Taking targeting lessons from these brands and TWISTING them to inspire your own targeting choices can be one of the most important things you do for your own brand. As we discussed in the 4 Key Questions, it all begins with the "who."

Create A Target Persona To Help Focus Your TWIST

Identifying an ideal target and knowing what makes them tick is not just important for large businesses. It's critical, perhaps even more so, for the small business owner because massive budgets aren't typically available.

In Brand School you identify your target by creating a target persona. You create fully fleshed-out characters giving them names, ages, number of children, pets, and marital status. You explore their lives broadly: what keeps them up at night, what was the last fight with a family member about, what made their favorite vacation so special? Only when you really recognize them do you start to probe what would make them receptive to hearing about and engaging with your products and services. As you put yourself in their heads, think about how they would explain their struggles in their own words.

Pay attention to the language your ideal target uses to describe themselves. One TWIST I love is from the website Abbey Post, which is an aggregator shopping site for full-figured women. Instead of using the term "full-figured" that feels like something created by a manufacturer, it refers to its targets as "curvy girls."

If you are targeting small business owners, for example, do they refer to themselves as a "small business owner?" Or are they more likely to say they are the "chief cook and bottle washer"? Listen for these nuances, and incorporate them into your branding to TWIST away from the competition.

> Adina, who is passionate about selling a unique water filtration system with proven science and lots of health benefits, was having trouble getting people to listen to her spiel. Of course everyone wants to be healthier, but this benefit is promised in so many categories, we tune it out. She used the Brand School framework to really understand her ideal target, the "who," and what was keeping them up at night. She shifted her opening lines from, "Hi. I am here to sell you healthy water," to "I can help keep you from taking 60 pills a day by the time you are 60." And the sales started flooding in.

Defined Targets Lead To Stronger Brand Promises

Here are a few examples of Brand School target TWISTS that are clearly defined, and thus can be used to create brand promises (the "what") that really break through and connect.

Instead of a mom looking for a creative activity to do with her kids:

A mom who is tired of her children always looking down at their various screens in the car and who thinks she might scream if they ask to play the video "Frozen" again in the minivan instead of talking to her or each other.

Instead of small business owners who need insurance:

Business people who are totally clueless about insurance, let alone knowing what kind they need.

Instead of small business owners who need business automation services:

Creative entrepreneurs who want to spend less time managing their business and more time doing the work they love.

Instead of people who want a more beautiful smile:

Middle-aged woman facing issues of self-identity as her children grow up and leave the nest, she wants to finally focus on her own needs.

Instead of anyone who would like to have a professional portrait shot:

Women who are re-entering the workforce after an extended period of time who are terrified of having their picture taken because they are sure they will hate what they see.

Instead of business owners who want to update their websites:

Entrepreneurs who have fallen out of love with their brands and want to feel reconnected and re-energized.

Do you see the difference in the examples above? By digging deeper, the targets shift from anonymous groups of people who could be anyone to real people that we can relate to, and then brand to, in a more specific and impactful way.

Here are a few of the sample questions we use when developing the target persona:

- What's keeping them up at night in relation to your category?

- What are they struggling with?

- What trade-offs are they currently making?

- What are they looking for but can't find?

- What have they tried before but been disappointed in?

Look For Your Target's Secret TWISTS

One TWIST you can try when creating these personas is to imagine something unusual or secret about your ideal target. Something that is fundamental to who they are but that they might not readily share. For example, what did they want to be when they grew up, what major did they really want to pursue in college, what would friends and colleagues be pleasantly surprised to find out about them?

These TWISTS make them more relatable and human and will help you find insights that really cut through.

> Lindsey and Charlie did this target persona exercise in a brand differentiation workshop and included the fact that their target, "Jim," a successful CEO, had actually grown up poor in a large family and had to depend on his church

and the goodwill of neighbors for hand-me-down clothes and other essentials. This fueled his intense desire to feel in control within his company. He didn't like to be at the mercy of other people or to be taken by surprise by shifts in the marketplace. So he was looking for a financial partner who would be proactive in his or her advice, staying ahead of the market and acting with tremendous transparency. They incorporated this target TWIST into one of their brand pillars that is about "dedicated teams."

Sometimes you will be surprised when you create a character and then end up meeting them in real life, which happened to me when I was working with the Virgin Charter brand. Virgin Charter was a new kind of marketplace where small charter companies could have access to people looking to rent planes. It was sort of an Orbitz for the private rental sector. We did this exercise and created a woman named Mary who owned a mom-and-pop charter service and was constantly worrying about not finding the right customers at the right time. I was attending a private aviation trade show in Savannah, Georgia, and "Mary" walked right into our booth, which really affirmed that we had done a thorough job of understanding our ideal target.

Targets Travel In Tribes Of Brand Ambassadors

When you connect with the right people who value your product, chances are much greater that they will have a positive user experience. In turn, they will want to shout about it to their friends in person, on Facebook, and or on broader platforms like Trip Advisor. These word-of-mouth recommendations are shown to be more believable and impactful than general messages directly from the brand – 75% of people surveyed don't trust ads and 71% are more likely to purchase based on social media referrals. [Source: Hubspot]

Another powerful thing about ideal targets is they tend to travel in tribes. For example, some tribes might be new moms looking for organic solutions, women entrepreneurs re-entering the workforce after taking time off, or sandwich generation women looking after elderly parents. This makes them easier to find and reach effectively and efficiently.

Mary was launching a unique business that refurbished old and unused pianos and transformed them into beautiful new objects such as bookshelves or bars. When she did a deep dive into her target's triggers for wanting to discard a piano, she realized that a lot of this activity was fueled by aging parents who were moving out of their large homes into smaller assisted-living apartments or nursing homes. The decision and conflict about what to do with a treasured family piano that was too big to move was often left to the adult daughters overseeing this transition. With this insight, she was able to target these decision-makers by acknowledging this emotional conflict and advertising her services with brands that were also targeting these "sandwich generation" daughters such as real estate brokers and support groups for people caring for aging parents. She tapped into her target's need to preserve memories in relationships that were

> transitioning with aging. These insights led to a successful brand idea of: "Create new beginnings for your family's grand memories" rather than a bland promise of "Get rid of your unwanted piano."

What Do You Do If You Have Multiple Ideal Targets?

Often I get pushback from students who say it's really difficult to pick only one target since their business relies on distinct target groups to make it work. For example, an educational product for teen boys that relies on moms to purchase it. Or an event planner that does both personal events like weddings and corporate events like fundraisers. Does this sound like your business? Do you have multiple targets? I address this by allowing up to three distinct targets, with one of these three designated as your primary target. Your primary target should be the one that is most essential in the sales process or that you would like to do more business with moving forward.

Create the target personas for each of these distinct targets and fill out the corresponding benefit pyramids mentioned previously. When you have finished the pyramids for each of your three targets, look for areas of commonality across them. You are looking for common motivators and desires. For example, a mom might be motivated by her child learning something while playing an educational game. The child might be motivated by winning and competition. While these might seem like different benefits, they both include an element of discovery and mastery that could be used in a common brand promise: "With X game, discover how far you can go."

If there is no reconciling your targets, and if you cannot find any common ground, then this is a sign you are reaching too broadly and cannot target them both under one brand. Most strong brands have one core brand promise even if they have multiple targets.

For example, Coca-Cola promises "Happiness" to kids, teens and adults alike but targets its marketing to each slightly differently. It recently designed a "friendly" bottle that can only be opened by another bottle and included this social packaging on college campuses to help college freshmen break the ice. But whether it is marketing to a ten year old or a forty year old, the core brand promise of "Happiness" remains constant.

Lynn was targeting both individuals and corporations with her unique art and movement therapy classes. She started with the assumption that these were two very different targets with very different needs. But after completing the personas and pyramids, she realized that although the first group was looking for self-improvement and the second group was looking to strengthen team-building skills, both of them were looking for more connections – to themselves and the people they interacted with. Thus she is now able to address both of them through a brand that promises to help them "Create a More Connected Life."

You Are Not Always Your Target – Look Through Their Eyes For The TWIST

While it is extremely important to create your target personas with as much detail as possible so you can identify strongly with them, it is also important to remember that you are not your target. Be careful to look at branding through their eyes, not your own. Often entrepreneurs start a business because they are trying to solve a problem that is very personal to them and one that they have experienced directly. However, sometimes the ideal target for the product or service is actually someone different from yourself.

> Michael created a new kind of gluten-free pancake for his daughter, who couldn't find anything she liked to eat on her restricted diet. While Michael was initially focused on nutrition, he made extra efforts to include a wide variety of flavor options because this was the key trigger for his pre-teen daughter who was easily bored. He was not his target, but he made sure to incorporate a key TWIST that was important to his audience.

TWIST With Your Favorite Brands

Think about the brands you would stand in line for, that you brag about to your friends, that you are willing to pay more for. What drives this connection and how can you TWIST these insights to strengthen your own branding?

Next time you come across a specific insight in an ad or website copy for one of your favorite brands, take a minute to really think what specific action or language they are using, and how you can apply it to your own branding.

For example, I love that the salespeople at Nordstrom come out in front of the counter to hand you your purchase. I think they really understand that their customer wants to feel good about the purchase they just made and would like to have that decision honored somehow. Observing this TWIST led to me change the way I welcome new students to Brand School and acknowledge the important investment they have just made in their brand. Instead of sending a welcome letter, I decided to give more tangible welcomes to Brand School students with a kit that includes a notebook and a folder where they can keep all their worksheets. I also decided to mark the important milestone of graduation with a certificate that is signed and mailed to them at the completion of the class.

TWIST With A Brand Your Target Already Loves

Another productive TWIST exercise is to choose a brand experience that your target admires (not necessarily one that you admire personally) and TWIST best practices of this brand to innovate your own. For example, if you have a clothing line targeting teen girls, but you are not one yourself, think about other brands and experiences they love. Your target might be crazy about a brand like Great Adventure, an amusement park that offers extreme thrill-seeking rides, something many adults would pass on by. Think about what's driving the teenager's love of this brand, and then TWIST those key drivers with your own brand. How could you incorporate the "thrill" of an amusement park ride into your online experience? Perhaps an interesting TWIST would be to have a "bonus wheel" that the teen shopper would spin each time for the thrill of a surprise free gift with purchase.

Conduct A Brand Experience Audit

A wonderful way to get rich feedback on your target is to do a brand experience audit. This is an audit of your brand journey – from initial research through purchase – done by a third party. This is a great exercise for an intern or to reciprocate with a friend who is also a small business owner. In Brand School we do this as a reciprocal exercise with a brand buddy, another student that you are paired with during the semester for added support and accountability.

These audits look at all key phases of the experience from discovery, purchase, usage, and even the time when you are not actively in the market but could be influencing others.

Here are a few sample questions from an audit:

- Is the brand easy to find online in a Google search?

- Are there other similar sounding brands that come up in the search?

- When you get to the website is it easy to navigate?

- Do you understand right away the brand idea (promise)?

- Is the promise purely functional or does it make you feel something as well?

- Do you have an idea who this brand is targeted to?

- What are your impressions of the look and feel of the site?

- Does it appear distinctive for the category? Or does it use colors/imagery that you would expect for that type of business?

These brand experience audits are a very common tool for agencies to use with corporate clients. However, they are rarely conducted for small businesses, which need them the most. Small businesses need to make sure their experiences are seamless, easy, and don't require a customer support team to help with service recovery.

Ed was opening a fertility clinic. To help, I decided to use my yearly physical with my own general doctor as an opportunity to do a brand experience audit during a generic medical visit to give him some valuable input. I used screen grabs on my computer and my cell phone camera to document and share my experience. Along the way I made notes about how I was feeling and what could be improved. One of the biggest "a-ha" moments for me was the realization that there was a missed opportunity in the examination room. In general, I really like my medical practice. They are professional, and most of the time live up to their brand promise of "compassion, confidence and commitment," except in one key area – the examination room. My doctor's exam room is small and functional, with one small hook on the back of the door to hang your clothes. As I piled my coat, blouse, skirt and tights on to this teeny hook, I realized this was an area where my experience was not

> matching the brand promise. No matter how neatly I tried to arrange the clothes, they looked like a big mess. If the medical practice really wanted to be "compassionate" why not give me a small locker to store my clothes? I shared this observation with Ed and he decided to provide an alternative storage TWIST to his target as he designed the offices for his clinic.

Your Ideal Target Will Pay More For Your Brand TWIST

Creating a tight ideal target means customers will be less price-sensitive because they have fully bought into your brand idea. Nearly all of our Brand School students end up raising their prices once they go through the class. Why? Because they connect with the right people who want their goods or services. And they are able to articulate more clearly a unique and relevant brand idea to those people.

> Margaret, a photographer, rebranded from a generic website that focused on her services (which were similar to many other events photographers) to one that clearly defined that she is the right choice for people not just looking for pretty pictures of their special day, but those customers who are looking for "exceptional images with an extra edge." Once she became clearer on her ideal target, she was able to attract clients who were willing to pay prices that were more in line with her rich experience. She let the bargain-hunters find another resource.

CHAPTER 5:
WALK YOUR BRAND TALK, BRING YOUR TWIST TO LIFE

The expression "actions speak louder than words" has taken on a whole new level of importance as consumers have become jaded by many brands that over-promise and under-deliver. What's the best way to connect with your targets? Show them you mean business by delivering on moments that matter. Addressing the what, why and how will mean that your target understands your product or service and will ultimately buy into what you are offering.

Put Your Money Where Your Mouth Is

These actions can be both large and small. Sometimes they are billion dollar gestures such as when CVS decided to back up its brand claims of "health is everything" by discontinuing sales of cigarettes in all 7,700 CVS locations nationwide. This may seem like an obvious action for a company rebranding itself from a pharmacy to a healthcare partner, but it's not without significant financial consequences. At the time, the company estimated that the decision would cut its overall sales by $2 billion, a necessary action to back up the words in the company's brand positioning. [Source: *USA Today*]

These actions can also be smaller moments of magic like the "Real Facts" on the underside of the Snapple juice caps that help reinforce their brand's positioning as a refreshing alternative to traditional soft drinks.

Here's a great example from Bissell, the vacuum cleaner company. All vacuums will say they do a superior job of cleaning, but Bissell is one of the few brands to show this with a very dramatic TWIST. A recent Bissell ad shows an employee down in the subway (undeniably one of the dirtiest places on earth), cleaning part of the subway platform with a Bissell vacuum and then eating his pasta lunch directly off the floor! This may be a bit exaggerated, but that's just the point. By taking an extreme situation, Bissell is demonstrating the superior cleaning power of its product. If it can get the subway platform that clean, just think what it can do for your kitchen. Bissell did another clever thing in this spot. At the end of the video the man eating off the platform is identified as a brand manager from Bissell and from this statement and the reactions of the subway riders around him, you can tell that this is a real event, not something staged with actors.

Visualize Your TWIST

When I worked for Virgin we used to call this dramatic visual storytelling the "money shot." Imagine your business is on the front cover of a national branding magazine and your brand has just won "Brand of the Year." You have a full-page cover designed to show, not tell, what your brand has done to prove its meaningful differentiation – its TWIST. What's the money shot? Start with that, and work your way back.

> Lenore works for a non-profit that provided greeting cards with inspirational messages of faith, love and concern. In our "Brand of the Year" exercise, she went way beyond the goal of distributing more cards to a much bigger ambition of using the cards to start a national "Kindness Movement." She envisioned the company's TWIST as thousands of people wearing "Kindness Matters" t-shirts on an appointed day and used this vision to hone and differentiate the organization's brand idea.

When I was part of the team launching Virgin Money (a peer-to-peer lending service) in Boston, we decided our money shot would be Richard Branson firing huge cannons filled with red paper dollars (Virgin's signature color) with his face on the dollar bill in downtown Copley Square. This was to signal a revolution in lending and how Virgin was "changing the face of money." This dramatic shot was featured on the cover of financial service sections of dozens of prominent national newspapers the next day, helping spread the word of the launch.

Your money shot doesn't need to be as dramatic as cannons going off, but it could be a signature photo or demonstration that is featured on your website or marketing materials that helps you stand out and be remembered.

Make Your TWIST "Word of Eye" Worthy

This visualization of your brand's TWIST is even more important now that we live in a world driven by social media. Think about all the images of brands and brand experiences that are posted to Twitter, Instagram and Pinterest. It's a new phenomenon that I call "word of eye." Years ago I would send a postcard to friends and family telling them about my vacation. Today, this seems archaic. Now I am more likely to take a picture with my cell phone of my hotel room, unusual lobby or the cool pool and post it within seconds to social media. Yesterday's "word of mouth" is now today's "word of eye." The bottom line is that companies today, both large and small, must ensure that their brand experiences are click, shoot and send-worthy.

A great example of "word of eye" at work is the Virgin America airline cabins. These cabins are specially equipped with one-of-a-kind mood lighting in multiple shades that adapt to outside light. This TWIST is seen as soon as you board the plane, when passengers immediately notice the purple glow and realize that this is not your typical airline. You can hear the oohs and aahs of the flyers and the clicks of cell phones as they snap pictures to share with their friends. And because the entire Virgin America fleet is wi-fi enabled, often these pictures are shared immediately during the flight – it's "word of eye" at 35,000 feet. Even small businesses can make a strong visual impression.

> Benan's brand name for her jewelry business means tulip in Turkish. She hands out tulip bulbs along with her business card in beautiful small gossamer sacks when she meets new people at gift and craft fairs.

TWIST The Overlooked Moments That Matter

A great way to "show, don't tell" in branding is to use the moments that other brands have overlooked and TWIST them to your advantage. Many small businesses feel they are never going to be able to shine in their markets because they don't have budgets for the big gestures like television ads or prominent billboards. But bigger isn't always better. In branding, it's often the small, overlooked, magic moments that cut through.

One of the things I admire about Richard Branson is his philosophy that "surprise and delight" gestures are key to brand-building and forming deep connections with customers. Today, Virgin is a large global brand, but in 1970 it was a small mail order record company and then a retail record store. At that time, Virgin presented an alternative to the formal, stuffy music atmospheres of traditional music retailers. Virgin Megastores were among the first music retailers to install listening booths so customers could "try before you buy." Over 40 years later, Virgin still tries to "surprise and delight" when entering new markets.

One of my favorite "surprise and delight" moments at Virgin is a promotion they did on Virgin Atlantic when they used the vomit bags in the seat pockets as marketing messages. These bags are an FAA requirement in every seat back on every flight. But they are usually plain white and a missed opportunity – right in front of passengers for the six-plus hour flight. Virgin Atlantic branded the bags its signature red, and included engaging copy about how flying used to be fun, then became terrible, and Virgin's mission was to make it fun again. It began with: "How did air travel become so bloody awful? First, they took away the meals. Then the pretzels. And then the peanuts. All seven of them …." It ended with: "Flying should make you feel like you are a virgin again (flying-wise of course). It should feel new. And on Virgin Atlantic Airways it always will."

How can you find your vomit bag moment?

Think About the End-To-End Brand Experience To Find Your TWIST

Many businesses make the mistake of thinking about pleasing their consumers only in the key moments when they are buying or using the brand. But you also need to think of moments early on in the decision process and in the moments when your target is no longer actively involved with your brand because even between purchases, your target can still be a great brand ambassador.

Engaging your target in these moments is key. Where does your brand experience really begin and end? Is it just when people are purchasing or actively interacting with your brand? How about the research phase? Or much earlier on in the process when they are only thinking about what they need? Or later in the process when they've had a great experience but might not be actively in the market again for a while? How can you keep in touch, stay top-of-mind, and add value during this down time? Or what about sharing the behind-the-scenes journey of the product they are ordering as it is being manufactured? People love an insider's view. It seems like many of the "making of x movie" specials we see on TV are just as popular as the actual finished movies.

Be on the lookout for brands that really make use of the whole experience. What can your business TWIST and learn from them?

One of the perks of working at Virgin was that I got to fly Virgin Atlantic every few months to visit the home office in London. I love that Virgin Atlantic looks at the whole continuum of the flight experience and not just the time you are in the air. For example, upper class flyers are picked up in a Virgin limousine, driven to the airport, checked in through a Virgin-only security channel and then have time to relax in a Virgin Clubhouse before the flight. These Clubhouses are not your average airport lounge. Here you can have amazing full service dining and spa treatments, work out, or get a haircut at the Bumble and Bumble salon. Once on board the flight, you can pass the time chatting with friends at the on-board bar.

But it's not just big statements like these that Virgin makes, there are also smaller touches like the salt and pepper shakers that look like mini-airplanes and are branded with the words "pinched from Virgin Atlantic" on the bottom with a nod to the many customers who can't resist taking them home as souvenirs. Once they land in someone's kitchen they continue to build brand awareness as curious houseguests turn them over and enjoy the same moment of delight as you did.

In Brand School, we spend a lot of time thinking about these small gestures that can really make a big difference. Pay attention to other brands, in different categories, that are making the most of their moments. We encourage students to keep a TWIST notebook and collect examples of "magic moments" and how they can inspire your brand. Once you start paying attention to the TWISTS, you will see great examples everywhere.

One "magic moment" that made a big impression on a CEO and BrandTwist client was a personalized thank you note sent from Mickey after his wife and teenage daughter went on a Disney vacation. This small gesture made a huge impact on him. He sent me a photograph of it and vowed to look for similar magic moments in his own brand continuum, which was in asset management. His business couldn't have been further away from Disney but he recognized the power of this TWIST and wanted to learn from it and apply it to his own brand with more customized marketing materials.

Rachel created an interesting TWIST to the traditional referral thank you note that many businesses send current clients for introducing them to new ones. Instead of the expected letter, bottle of wine, or gift card, she decided to do something that stood out and was really on brand for her. Her design company targets entrepreneurs who have fallen out of love with their branding. Her aim is to get the conversation started again, to help them remember why they started their own business in the first place and eventually to channel that reignited passion into a new design. In keeping with the conversation theme of her brand idea, she created "chatter box" gift sets to say thank you for referrals. These are simple cardboard boxes filled with small personalized gifts and a note that says: "Thank you for being a chatter box and introducing me to so and so...." This TWIST was inspired by Starbucks, which she loves and admires for how they customize their drinks. Her local Starbucks knows her and can make her drink without her even ordering. She wanted to reward her referrals by customizing a box of their favorite things. It's a simple, magic

> moment that really stands out. She is going to thank her referrers anyway, but now does it in a way that reminds them of her brand TWIST.

When you notice a magic moment of a favorite brand, think about what's engaging you in that moment. For example, is it a funny word on a packaging slip or invoice, clever on-hold music, or a different kind of message when your computer has timed out? Why did this gesture stand out? Chances are these are moments that other brands missed and this brand has taken the opportunity to turn that moment into an emotional connection with a unique TWIST.

Another example of a magic moment you can TWIST with is the Amazon smile box (the simple brown box with the big smile on the outside). This is an excellent example because it underscores that the best moment in the Amazon process is when you actually receive what you ordered and it is acknowledging and sharing in your happiness. The smile also begins under the A in Amazon and ends at the Z. This visual TWIST underscores the "A to Z" nature of Amazon that has such a wide variety of goods and services.

> Candice designed an app that targeted moms with children with Attention Deficit Hyperactivity Disorder (ADHD) and created a yearly calendar with time and stress saving tips around each important holiday and milestones in their children's year (i.e., back to school, holiday breaks) to offer 360-degree support. This was a unique TWIST because it was outside of the gamification learning app, but at the same time fit great

> with her brand and the core brand promise of helping moms to help their kids thrive and "Own Proud." When you buy the app you also get access to a community that provides quick, healthy recipes; tips from moms and experts to help your child with school; inspiration and support; and stories of proud moments from other families. This 360-degree approach to ADHD support is a unique TWIST in this market, which usually is very sub-specified. This gains her not only users of the app, but loyal fans who will recommend it to other families.

What's the best moment in your customer's journey and how can you celebrate it with them? Completing a brand experience audit or mapping the brand journey from start to finish is a great way to bring these opportunities to light. The trick is to focus on all of the moments along the brand journey, not just the ones where the consumer is engaged or the brand is in control.

Business-to-Business Brands Can Leverage TWISTED Moments Too

I use the email subscriber MailChimp to manage my subscriptions and mailing list. As part of their services, they send me an email whenever someone joins or unsubscribes to my mailing list. This is a standard service that all email managers provide; however, MailChimp does it in a way that reinforces their brand TWIST of being a friendly, easy-to-manage platform for businesses.

The new subscriber alert I receive reads: "Nice! Guess people like what you're saying." While the copy on the unsubscribe alert reads: "Bummer. These things happen for a number of reasons…." This reassures me that things are still under control, and then goes on to give me a link with some useful tips on keeping my mailing list healthy. It's the use of the word "bummer" that really stands out for me. It's just what I am thinking in my head and it makes me smile and softens the rejection moment. It's also a unique and refreshing TWIST for a business-to-business brand. This small gesture, and other touches like the MailChimp funky monkey logo, is why they stand out among their competition with "a splash of mischief to a product category not known for… well, much of anything." [Source: *Fast Company Magazine*]

Challenge Category Norms To Maximize The Impact Of Your TWIST

Looking for vomit-bag moments is also about challenging category norms. Just because things have always been done a certain way, does it mean it has to continue that way? At Virgin, they are committed to shaking things up, and a big part of that is questioning the "givens" in a category. Having an outside point of view present also does this. Virgin's business development teams are always made up of both people who have deep category experience and those that are "virgins," who might be new to the category.

For example, when I was working on creating Virgin Hotels we questioned every assumption about hotels, their design, and functionality and why certain things (like room layout) were always the same. We approached the experience from a customer point of view – and not only as operators. The result? The Virgin Hotel that launched in Chicago has a unique room layout that divides the standard hotel room into two distinct living zones: the dressing room and the sleeping lounge. It also features interior privacy doors so room service can be delivered without disturbing your conference call or catching you just out of the shower. There is also a patent-pending hybrid bed with an ergonomic headboard and erectable footboard that allows guests to "Work comfy, lounge lavishly, and rest like modern royalty." The headboard has been designed with plush, lower lumbar support so you can work against it with a laptop. This is a vast improvement from the standard hotel work desks that are never conveniently located and uncomfortable. Virgin knows its customers are tech savvy and probably want to be comfortable working on their laptops, so they redesigned the bed to make this easier.

Often challenging these norms can provide a better target experience and save your company money because you are redirecting funds to moments that really count. When I was at Virgin Management, Virgin Atlantic realized it was often cost-prohibitive to offer amenity kits to first and business class customers. Many people opened the kits and removed one or two items they liked, which led to a tremendous amount of expensive product waste. They experimented with walking around cabins with large wicker baskets so customers could choose the items they want. This was a better practice from an operational standpoint for the airline, and it felt more personal to the customers.

Try dropping any preconceived notions of the way things "have to be or have always been" in your industry. Think instead from the point of view of your customer and what would make his or her experience better.

Engage Overlooked Senses To TWIST

Finding moments to TWIST is really about using the whole brand journey and engaging all of the senses. We often market to people's sight, but what about the other senses?

The Book Midwife writing, coaching and publishing company sends its authors downloadable tracks of music that they have specifically chosen with lengths and rhythms that are ideal for productive and inspired writing. The InterContinental Hotels Group uses signature scents in its hotel properties that are catered to a specific target guest's needs and expectations. They believe that fragrance branding helps increase brand loyalty.

What senses are your brand overlooking? For example, could you send a client a playlist of music that reminds them of the experience of working with your brand?

Promote And Celebrate TWISTS You Are Already Providing

Look at your own brand. Maybe you are already providing some add-on services, but are not really thinking of them as part of your core brand offering. Talk to your potential customers about the support you provide before, during, after the purchase, as well as the down times between active engagements. Make a list of the "extras" that you are consistently doing but not necessarily touting or charging for. These may seem like givens to you, but chances are your competitors are not doing many of them and this would be a great area to TWIST. A brand experience audit will also highlight these areas. It will be able to pick up on those leverageable "hidden extras" that have become second nature to you. You don't always have to charge extra for these TWISTS, but it could be a very good idea to start talking about them as a point of differentiation. Often these extras have to do with accessibility. Do you deliver products to customers when they can't get to you? Give clients your home phone number? Provide introductions to other clients informally or formally? These are all great examples of "showing, not telling" that you are committed to client service.

> Rachel, who works for a test and college prep business, realized that one of its TWISTS was to broker introductions and visits between former clients now in college and current high school students in the midst of the search process. She realized this service was an extension of the brand's commitment to help students thrive and was an important benefit. She now highlights it as one of the company's TWISTS.

Downtime Can Be A Great Time To TWIST

When you are keeping in touch with your past customers in some of the down periods, make sure you are doing so with useful information and connections. Social media is a great tool to fuel brand engagement on an ongoing basis.

For example, we have a private Facebook page for Brand School alumni called the BHIVE. We use this page to help continue the conversation around branding topics but also to encourage former students to refer clients to each other and often to create joint offerings. It's not just a hub of information, it's also a new business tool. Keeping former students engaged also keeps us top-of-mind and helps prompt referrals for future classes.

How do you keep that engagement and show, not tell, that your brand is really different when it comes to creating strong relationships with your customers? A lot of this has to do with the idea of "surprise and delight" and doing the unexpected by saying yes when other brands typically say no.

For example, maybe you are asking your customers to fill out a feedback survey. But are you really following up on their feedback? Are you letting them know they've been heard and that you are doing something about it?

Recently, my friend Bonnie stayed at a nationally-known wellness spa and filled out the standard post-stay survey. She mentioned in the comments that she found the food was not as good as in previous visits. Imagine her surprise when she got a call from the executive chef who spent 30 minutes talking to her about her specific comments and suggestions. Now that's walking the talk.

Here's an ultimate example of "surprise and delight" while "walking the talk." Cade Pope, a twelve-year-old NFL fan sent a letter to the owner of each of the NFL's 32 teams asking for help deciding which team he should support. He received only one response – a handwritten letter from Jerry Richardson, the Carolina Panthers owner. The letter stated, "Cade, we would be honored if our Carolina Panthers became your team. We would make you proud by the classy way we represent you." The letter also came with a package containing a replica Panthers helmet signed by star linebacker Luke Kuechly. Pope said: "If this is the only team that responds to me, I'm a Carolina Panthers fan."

To me this story represents the power of asking for business using a personal touch with an impactful TWIST. What's the big deal of gaining one twelve-year-old fan? Assuming he's going to stay a Panther's fan for life, that's a pretty savvy investment. Plus, in the world of social media, these kinds of stories usually go viral. This story got over 104,000 likes on Facebook and thousands of tweets and comments that built brand recognition and feel-good fan moments along the way.

How can your brand learn from these examples and provide an authentic and unexpected TWIST to really show your customers that you care? Most of the time, it is simply about taking the time to say thank you and we hear you, in an authentic and personal way. This can be an advantage for small businesses as chances are you actually know your clients.

> Jean has a business where she helps creative entrepreneurs "Drive Their Dreams Forward" by providing them with market overviews and support to build strong business plans. When her client engagements are finished she provides them with a USB drive that has the TWIST of being shaped like a key (a nod back to her drive forward theme). On it she puts all of the files from the work they did together and often some added bonuses such as relevant trend presentations. Her clients, who are overwhelmed entrepreneurs building their new businesses while still working full time, really appreciate this gesture and the unique way it is delivered.

Mind The Gaps: Make Sure You Deliver On Your TWIST

While actions speak louder than words, they also need to be in alignment with each other. You need to mind the "gaps" between what your brand is promising and how you (and your staff) are actually behaving.

Have you ever had a doctor tell you that you really need to eat healthier and lose some weight, and you can't really concentrate on what he is saying because you are too distracted by his belly protruding from under his white coat? This is an example of a gap between messaging and behavior that can undermine brand credibility. What about a restaurant that spends lots of money telling you about its commitment to freshness through print and in-house advertising but then you find the restroom dirty and unkempt. It erases a lot of the restaurant's hard-spent budget and makes you question how its words actually translate into action.

Ask yourself where your gaps might be. For example, do you spend a lot of time talking about how you really listen to your client's needs, and then go into a new business pitch showcasing your own capabilities while overlooking the research you've done on your client? Try TWISTING this by sending a pre-meeting survey with the question: "What would be most helpful to you for us to share during the precious and limited time we have to get to know each other?"

Have you touted your innovative approach to problem-solving and then went into a meeting with the same uninspired presentation tools that everyone else is using? If the above sounds familiar, it is time to go back to your brand idea and pillars. The pillars can help drive how you behave, not just speak, and really bring your brand to life through actions that support your promises.

> Erik is a talented musician and the CEO of a small recording studio and sound engineering business that employs nine people in Manhattan. Once he finished Brand School and was satisfied with his new and improved brand story, Erik made a point of sharing it with his employees. Not just once but in monthly status meetings. They reviewed what the company stood for and how it was different – the TWIST – and talked about how the employees were bringing this story to life in their daily interactions with customers. They also identified areas where there were gaps between what they were promising and how they were behaving. For example, they were talking about the ability of the company to offer complete solutions, but then they realized that many of their customers only knew about one aspect of their services – for example, recording – but didn't realize that they also did original compositions. This was partly because the company had different brand names for each service. They changed the brand architecture and put the three different divisions under the single master brand name. This made it easier to offer their clients all of their services and deliver on their core brand TWIST of "Your vision at the speed of sound."

In my own business, I use my BrandTwist pillars to help me create new products, services, and specific content. For example, I speak three to four times a month to different groups of entrepreneurs, small businesses and non-profits on a range of branding issues. Often I am faced with the best way to use the "stage" time I have been given. When in doubt, I use my pillars as a guide.

My brand pillars are:

Interactive – I always find ways to get the audience involved so I am not just talking for an hour.

Lateral – I bring in lots of TWISTS and when possible try to have the room configured in a unique way or pick an out-of-the-ordinary venue.

Actionable – I always make sure that the attendees leave with a few ideas that they can implement right away to strengthen their brands and businesses.

Build your pillars into your fundamental business practices.

Build An Internal Culture That TWISTS

Finally, showing not telling is a big part of being an effective leader and building a strong internal brand culture. Remember, your employees are your best brand ambassadors. But to fill this role they really need to embody your brand pillars. And effectively modeling that brand involvement begins with you.

Observe other brands that you admire and delve into what makes their employees such strong brand ambassadors. What can you learn from the blue shirts at the Apple store or the baristas at Starbucks? What gestures (large and small) make those interactions so on-brand and how can you TWIST and get inspired to strengthen your employee culture (even if the employee is just you!)?

This is an area where you also need to conduct a gap analysis between your brand idea and pillars, and your behavior and that of your employees. For example, is your brand promising to help people achieve balance in their lives but your own internal work/life balance is out of control? Are you sending employees emails on the weekends and during vacation, while espousing a philosophy of balance? Even if you say "don't respond until Monday," chances are they will respond earlier or at least be thinking about it, when they need the precious weekend time to recharge. Why not put the email in a "to send" folder and actually send it on Monday or when they are back from vacation? That's walking your brand talk, internally.

CHAPTER 6:
TRAIN YOUR BRAIN TO TWIST

Looking for and applying the TWIST taps into my core belief that consumers don't live in a one-category world. They make note of great brand experiences across airlines, retail stores, hair salons, fast food, fine dining, taxi cabs, doctors' offices, and personal trainers to name a few. As branders and entrepreneurs we should constantly be looking at the larger brandscape for inspiration. A key to successful TWISTING is to imagine what a beloved brand in a different category would do if it took over your business. How would this brand use its brand DNA to innovate in your market? By TWISTING an inspirational brand (i.e., Virgin, Zappos, Starbucks, Apple) with your brand you can create fresh and actionable ideas for your business.

My Brand School students TWISTED Starbucks with Delta Airlines. Ideas that came out of this TWISTING challenge were: writing passenger names on small blackboards on the top of the headrest of each seat like the baristas do on the coffee cups. Evolve the seat-back tray tables to keep up with the way people work and entertain themselves today with laptops and tablets. One inspired student suggested redesigning the tray tables so they actually fit a laptop with a cup holder for coffee or a drink. Many students suggested having more casual, café style seating instead of rows of people facing the same direction.

Even though this isn't feasible from an operational standpoint, Delta did, in actuality, create an unusual community with the 2014 launch of "Innovation Class." Innovation Class is a mentoring program that takes place 35,000 feet in the air. Leaders in business, art and technology agree to use the flight to mentor the person in the seat next to them. These Innovation Class seats are applied for over LinkedIn and are designated for entrepreneurs, or what Delta dubs the "new generation of innovators." This TWISTING initiative allows Delta to demonstrate a fresh idea and align themselves with the entrepreneur community, which resulted in positive press exposure.

A key thing to note here is that none of these Starbucks/Delta TWIST examples included a suggestion to "serve better coffee on board." That would be an easy fix, and maybe even a good co-branding opportunity, but it's low-hanging fruit and not ownable. This is branding at the bottom of the pyramid. It's a focus on attributes and not big, distinctive ideas. So many hotels now include a sign in their lobbies by the coffee machines that they are serving Starbucks coffee that it is no longer a distinguishing feature, and definitely not a driver of choice and loyalty from one hotel over the next.

Guidelines For TWISTING With Impact

When TWISTING with another brand to innovate for your business, there are a few important guidelines. Feel free to use national or local brands, as long as they inspire you and cause you to think or experience something meaningful.

1. **First choose a brand that you know and like** – you need to have positive experiences and a reasonable knowledge of that brand to draw on.

2. **Make sure that brand is NOT in a category related to yours** – if you make gourmet jam, don't pick Whole Foods – in fact the further away from your category the better.

3. **Choose a brand that has addressed a challenge that you are also facing in your business.** For example, you might choose Virgin because it has been able to shake up a tired market, or Netflix because it reinvented the movie viewing experience, or Disney because you love the magical, emotional connection it has with its consumers.

4. **Delve into all the magic moments, big and small, that make that brand special** – get as specific as possible. For example, if you are TWISTING with Apple, make a list of all the distinctive elements from the blue-shirted employees, the hand-held checkout, the Genius Bar in the stores, the unique intuitive touch screens, and the anticipated and orchestrated product releases.

5. **Pretend this inspirational brand took over your business** – what would they add, transform and change? It's useful to be as specific as possible. Don't just say: "Starbucks would make my dry-cleaning business more customized." Go further and think through the idea. Maybe you would have a large services menu displayed at the front of the store displaying daily specials or different "sizes" of starch.

6. **Draw and describe in detail one or two of your favorite ideas and write down three steps to move this idea forward.** In order for your ideas to become a reality, you need to go deeper into how they would work

and have a clear action plan for next steps. Drawing your idea and explaining it in a paragraph helps to make sure it is fully formed. The next steps should be small and actionable and include specific dates for completing tasks. In the dry-cleaning "menu" idea above they might include: 1) list out services that could be included in the menu; 2) two hours of online research into chalk board displays for purchase; 3) create a production plan and budget by a fixed target date.

TWISTING Takes Practice And Planning

TWISTING is an impactful practice, but it takes discipline and planning to actively seek it out and leverage it in your business-building activities. To effectively disrupt your normal thought patterns and business habits takes conscious effort. However, once you become aware of your autopilot behaviors and change them, you can have tremendous impact with TWISTING.

A few years ago I came across an article in a woman's magazine that encouraged women to practice more mindful eating by using their left hands. The article said if you are normally right-handed, make an effort to break out of this pattern and eat with your left hand and you will have more control over what you eat. After repeated forced use of your less dominant side, not only does willpower improve, but overall complex task mastery improves as well.

It got me thinking about other autopilot behaviors that may be inadvertently limiting your perspective and tightening your brand blinders. TWISTING helps you go beyond these self-imposed category constraints to create branding solutions that will stand out and get noticed.

TWIST Out Of Your Daily Routine

The first step in breaking out of the routine is learning to identify some of the habits you are unconsciously following. It's a great idea to keep a "business activity journal" for a week. Take note on an hourly basis of what you do. Begin with your morning routines, the things you do before you even get to work: what you have for breakfast, what newspaper you read or radio stations you listen to, what route you take to work. Where do you sit in the office, who do you chat with, what time do you take your coffee breaks, how often do you check your email, etc.? Just record, don't judge, for a week. Then look for patterns and behaviors you can shake up.

Look at each of these items and come up with at least one TWIST, one new way of approaching this task. For example, if you usually sit at a desk in one area of your office, try sitting somewhere else. This could mean moving your chair, trading desks with someone else, or going out of the office to work. Or try something as simple as rearranging the objects/photos on your desk, or my favorite, sitting under your desk on the floor! It's amazing how this new physical perspective will open up new mental pathways.

If this seems daunting, then start small. Commit to one day a week to change up one thing in your routine. I like to do this on Tuesdays, which I call TWISTING Tuesdays. This alliteration reminds me to schedule this lateral thinking. It's also the day I publish our "Brands That TWIST" blog post on BrandTwist.com that looks at a brand that is doing something unusual to shake up its category.

Team Up To TWIST

TWISTING is also a great activity to do with someone else. At Brand School, one of the most important success elements is partnering up our students with a brand buddy for weekly support and input. Here are a few ideas of what you can do with your buddy:

- Conduct a brand experience audit on each other's business.

- Introduce each other to a new passion – such as a TV show, musician, or restaurant.

- Trade places for the day and actually exchange offices.

- Confide in each other about a work or personal activity that intrigues but intimidates you, and then create a plan together to master it (like public speaking or zumba dancing).

- Give each other an assignment to read a section of the newspaper that you don't normally read and then report back on one story. Challenge each other to think how it can relate to your business.

This brand buddy system works great at an individual peer level. You could also consider hiring a coach or selecting a mentor to help you get out of your comfort zone. If you do this, make sure you pick someone you admire, but who also has qualities you don't possess. If your objective is to broaden your approach and horizons, you don't want someone exactly like you.

For example, a few years back I joined a coaching group based out of Southern California that focused on helping "heart-centered" entrepreneurs build their businesses. While I think I am a pretty nice person, I've always defined myself as more "head-centered" than "heart-centered." The practices of this group such as meditation and using incense were out of my comfort zone. But I decided I needed to follow my own TWISTING advice, and break out of the networking habits of associating only with people who were just like me. In the end, they taught me new perspectives, and the experience made me a better listener and a more empathetic teacher. I am glad I have these new tools to draw on and TWIST as I see fit.

TWIST The Types Of People You Interact With

We tend to network with like-minded people who speak our language and share our expertise and point of view. This can be important but often it has limited return on your investment of time. To shake things up you should actively seek out others with a different point of view. Consider joining Meetups (local networking meetings for similar interests) made up of people with different skills sets and points of view from your own. For example, instead of only going to networking events of women entrepreneurs, you could mix it up and attend some tech Meetups for web or app developers. This is especially important if technology is an area you are not comfortable with. You might meet some lovely digital natives who will give you advice/translations/resources on your key issues and also benefit from your business wisdom. You might even walk out with some ideas on how to pitch projects together or TWIST your skills for greater impact.

This is also a valid exercise when you are hiring employees or interns. Each year, I take an intern from our local high school. It's part of a senior program in the spring where the kids get real world experience and school credit, and local business owners get some free and valuable support. My habit the first few times was to seek out "mini-me's" – young women who were confident, extroverted and shared some of my favorite brands. But one year I decided to follow my own TWISTING advice and hire a young man who was a good student, interested in business, but somewhat shy. He introduced me to brands that I wouldn't normally know about, and he wrote a great guest blog post about Chipotle from the point of view of its core target audience: young men. He was hard-working and because he was slightly harder to get to know than those I usually hired, I found our professional relationship even more rewarding once it did develop. It also made me challenge my own behaviors. I came to realize that his quietness was a reflection of the fact that he was really listening and absorbing what was going on around him. This was a habit that I started to adopt with my own clients and students and it served me well on many projects. TWISTING the kinds of people we surround ourselves with can be a great source of inspiration.

TWIST Up Your Experts

Another impactful way to get "big picture" perspective and take off your category blinders is to TWIST up the experts that you go to for input on your business challenges. I was first exposed to a version of this technique when I did an "entrepreneur in residency" at a global innovation agency. I've since evolved it for my own work, which is fueled by the common insight that we tend to rely on the same expert sources, whether people we talk to in person, blogs or trade journals that we read. But using the same in-category experts leads to the same insights and does not often inspire lateral thinking or TWISTING.

A strategy to address this is to include random but related experts in your discovery process. For example, if you are branding a skincare product that has the main benefit of "protection," interview a corrections officer. This will give you fresh insights and language that is the opposite of what you would find in beauty magazines and websites. It might unlock some fresh thinking. If you are branding a new financial services product that offers maximum "flexibility", consult a choreographer or dancer to stretch your thinking. Or you can do more passive research by looking on websites of companies and organizations related to these activities and look for phrases, colors, concepts from these categories and TWIST them with your own brand.

TWIST Up Your Media

Deliberately read publications that are outside of your industry. Seek out magazines, blog posts and other media that appeal to the same target (i.e., sandwich generation baby boomers) but are not specifically in the category you are marketing in (i.e., financial services). Or better yet look at magazines that are as far away as you can get from your category and target (i.e., skateboard magazines for young boys if you are targeting baby boomers) in order to get fresh inspiration. This will drive a strong TWIST.

TWIST Your Tone

TWISTING your words is a great way to make sure that you are using fresh language and not falling into category jargon.

Verbal identity (the use of language to create a distinct brand impression) is an often overlooked part of branding even though it's a great opportunity for small business owners. Updating your visual identity (logo, website) often requires you to hire outside experts, but developing a unique tone of voice as a verbal TWIST is something you can often do on your own. The exact words you choose help communicate more than fact; they communicate brand personality.

Think about the scriptwriting in your favorite sitcoms or dramas. The writer has a character in mind when they write a line and is using language to communicate and reveal something about the character. For example, think about any scene from the popular HBO series *Sex in the City* where the four main characters, who are all very different personalities, are speaking about their dates the previous night. The way Charlotte describes a great evening out is very different from the way Samantha describes her evening. That's because each of these characters has been developed with a unique tone of voice.

How can you use tone of voice to make your brand shine? Think about brands you admire for their unique use of words – on websites, ads, product packaging, and social media. Collect and review their brand language and analyze what is special about each of these brands. Are they making you laugh, turning a phrase, adding a wink? Now try writing a headline for your brand by TWISTING it with the tone of voice from one of these brands. What is the effect? Are you using new language? Now try it again using a very different brand with a different tone for inspiration. Note the differences.

Virgin has a unique tone of voice that is often described as "cheeky." It is always focused on presenting information or benefits in a fun, fresh and engaging manner and never at the expense of the customer. For example, this announcement appeared on a gate board in San Francisco updating the passengers on a late departure to Washington, D.C.:

"Our aircraft is arriving late due to traffic restrictions here at SFO. Once the aircraft parks at the gate, a rabid badger will be released at the rear of the aircraft to encourage people to exit forward quickly. Once we have secured the badger and cleaned the cabin, we will board for D.C."

What do you think the impact of this copy was? My guess is that the passengers, having been kept up-to-date *and* amused, were probably a bit less grumpy when they boarded the "badger-free" plane.

Establishing your brand's unique tone of voice and then laying out guidelines on how and how not to communicate can be an effective tool for any small business building a tight and differentiated brand. It ensures every piece of written communication, no matter how big or small, is presenting a unified voice. It can also save a lot of time and money in that it allows you to outsource communications like tweets and press releases to other resources – freeing you up for more strategic tasks while ensuring that your brand voice is consistent.

TWIST Your Tagline

Another key piece of verbal identity is the tagline you use. Where would Nike be without "Just Do It" or Apple without "Think Different"? These are iconic taglines that encapsulate the brand's unique TWIST in just a few words.

> Ned has a wine school that TWISTS away from the traditional, often snobby, approach of wine appreciation toward a more social atmosphere where learning about wine becomes an integral part of enjoying life. He realized his tagline "enhance your appreciation and enjoyment of wine" didn't quite capture his TWIST. He changed it to "Uncork Your Joy of Living" which is shorter, more impactful and more telegraphic of his TWIST.

TWIST Away From Category Jargon

To stand out in your market you need to TWIST away from category jargon and acronyms. Every category has them. And often when you work in a certain area of business, you don't even notice when you are using them anymore. I call this jargon "ten dollar words." These are words that try too hard to be sophisticated. You may think they make you sound smart and serious, but often they confuse and intimidate your customer. Unless you are in a job where you need to sound erudite (an economist or a nuclear physicist) then "five dollar" words are usually a better bet.

Here are some examples:

Ten Dollar	Five Dollar
Achieve	Get
Provide	Give
Specialized	Different
Solutions	Answers
Concept	Idea
Effective	Works

If you are not sure if you are using them, it's a great idea to have someone who doesn't work for you or work in a similar type of business read your brochure or website copy and highlight any words that aren't 100% clear – words that fall into the acronym, jargon or the ten-dollar word trap.

A conversation I had with my son made me realize I was guilty of this with some of my Columbia University students and helped me to adjust my own language so it was more readily understandable for my graduate students. It also reinforced the importance of using tangible examples to bring the teaching points home.

One night after I came home from teaching an integrated marketing class, my son asked me what we had talked about in class. I told him we talked about "implementing effective promotion plans." This answer was met with a blank stare. I thought about how I could explain this concept to a tween and decided to relate it to an experience we had the year before when we were skiing in Colorado. While there, a national granola brand was passing out free granola bars at the entrance to the ski slopes. I reminded him about this and asked him whether he thought giving out those free samples would actually result in us buying those granola bars at the store. Was this an "effective promotion plan" for the granola company? He said no, since we couldn't buy them locally but then quickly started brainstorming ways that the granola people could increase the chances of the freebies leading to more paid sales, including the creation of a special ski helmet that came with a granola bar holder on top.

Bringing this concept down to the "five dollar" level for my son by throwing out jargon like "implementing effective promotion plans" and instead talking about "promotions that sell products" with a tangible example led to my own TWIST of making sure I talk to my students in a more real and useful way.

TWIST To Create Names That Stand Out

Try this TWIST technique when naming a new company, or new products and services. Isolate the features and benefits of the product or service, but change the category. For example, when I was working on a corporate client assignment to name a cell phone, I listed all the attributes of the phone (sleek design, catchy name, etc.) but put them in the context of a spirits product like a vodka. Instead of thinking about the phone name as something users would want to brag about to their friends, I thought about the vodka name needing to have a strong "bar call" and be something you feel cool asking the bartender for. This TWISTING technique helps you move away from the expected category language to something fresh and different.

Here's another useful technique when you are trying to name something. Instead of going right to the dictionary or thesaurus, surround yourself with magazines that have nothing to do with your business or category and circle key words and headlines that inspire you. Collect inspirational images as well. Look for words and images that capture the benefits and emotions that you want to express in your brand idea. Once you have collected these inspirational words and images, begin to create names. For example, if you have an image of a blue sky, use this to create names: Azura Coaching, Winged Wellness, White Dove Partners. This is a far more effective technique than starting in your category and looking at a thesaurus to find new ways of saying the same thing. In addition, traditional names will most likely be unavailable as a trademark or URL because someone else will already have thought of it. TWISTING your words to something more unique helps increase the chances of finding names that stand out and that you can trademark.

TWIST Up Your Partnerships

Strategic partnerships can be a great way to build your brand. To TWIST, actively seek out company from unlikely partnerships instead of going it alone. Teaming up with other brands that have common goals and visions, or different and complementary expertise, is a great way to grow your business and brand recognition.

In recent years, there have been some inspired product partnerships such as Nike and Apple that created the

Nike+iPod sports kit. This kit allows customers to insert a sensor in their Nike running shoes that "talks" to their iPod and creates a personalized playlist during their run. It also acts like a personal trainer by allowing them to access motivational sayings to keep their momentum up.

Nike CEO Mark Parker said this about the pairing: "Nike+iPod is a partnership between two iconic, global brands with a shared passion for creating meaningful consumer product experiences through design and innovation." [Source: Apple.com/pr/library] Small businesses can also learn to partner successfully by looking for other brands that share a similar point of view or address a similar target.

> Candice created a new app that helps kids with Attention Deficit Hyperactivity Disorder build focus through gamification and provides a non-medication treatment alternative. She decided to partner with other professionals (nutritionists and behavioral therapists) who were also targeting this market and believed in alternative approaches. She had them contribute content to her blog and spread the word of the game's launch to their customers, which expanded the impact of her launch.

The TWIST To Hire "On-Brand" Employees

Trusting your intuition on hiring decisions is also critical. As I've mentioned, employees are your most important brand ambassadors. How do you make sure you are choosing the right ones? Often we prioritize skill sets and experience over everything else. We want to make sure someone has a proven track record performing the tasks we are asking him or her to complete. Try this TWIST instead: hire for attitude and train for skill. Use your brand idea and pillars as an interview filter. Since one of my brand pillars is about lateral thinking (finding and applying the TWIST), I often ask candidates to tell me about a personal or professional situation where they created a solution that was non-traditional, more effective, and had a TWIST.

Hiring someone with the right brand values and behaviors who doesn't come from your industry can have other advantages as well. They can help you remove your brand blinders by bringing to the table insights and best practices from other categories that you can then TWIST to innovate and grow your business. Virgin has a strong employee culture of service and a can-do attitude; it often prioritizes attitude over in-category experience when looking for great employees. Richard Branson has said: "We look for passion, determination and quite a bit more…. The leaders we find all share the same entrepreneurial spirit and focus on customer service that are part of Virgin's DNA." [Source: entrepreneur.com.]

Get Out Of Your Office To TWIST

There is no substitute for getting out of your office and interacting with customers. Months into a project on pet food strategy at Interbrand, I realized that we were so busy doing desktop research and reading client-supplied documents that we had yet to come face-to-face with a real dog or their owner. I decided to change that. We went to Central Park in NYC and spent hours observing and interacting with dog owners at the dog park. We also arranged in-home interviews with a handful of new dog owners to talk to them about their habits and attitudes around feeding their dogs.

In one of these in-home interviews, we listened to a woman tell us quite rationally that she understood her new puppy was "just a dog." And that while she cared about his nutrition, she didn't go to the lengths she would in researching the same kind of food choices as she would for her children. It all sounded very reasonable and rational and convincing. However, as we sat with her for an hour, she had her new puppy in her lap the whole time. She spent that time petting him with the tenderness and attention you would give a newborn. While her words were saying one thing, her body language was clearly communicating a very different message: one of a very deep emotional attachment. This is the kind of insight we would have missed if we were not sitting with her and witnessing this first-hand. It was incorporated into the work we did with our client by reminding them to TWIST the scientific credentials of the product with the deep attachments people have for their pets.

Go TWIST On A Brand Safari!

One of my favorite TWISTING techniques is to go on a brand safari. Brand safaris are organized inspiration adventures. They can be done on your own or in groups and make fantastic activities for marketing off-site meetings, or just a great way to reframe your day. Many locations can be a source of inspiration, as long as they are out of your everyday routine and you are intentionally observing positive aspects of your experience and thinking about how you can TWIST them to build your brand.

Here are some of my favorite brand safari locations in New York City: MOMA, Build–A–Bear store on 5th Avenue, Ace Hotel lobby, Chelsea Market, Grand Central Terminal Shops, Lower East Side Tenement Museum, Nintendo World Store, the flagship Apple Store, and the M & M's retail store in Times Square.

If you are not sure where you would go on a brand safari where you live, here are some questions to ask yourself to help find ideal locations:

1. What are the local brand experiences that really engage people?

2. What's hot and why?

3. What's a best-kept local secret?

4. Where do all the kids or teens love to go?

5. Where do the tourists go in your town or city?

6. Where does the customer service exceed expectations?

Observe and record what is going on around you; bring a notebook or a clipboard with paper, take photographs, buy something from the store or location and see what the purchase experience is like. Notice the packaging. Do they give you your purchase in a plain paper or a plastic bag – or does the brand use the packaging as a walking billboard, like the Build–A–Bear cardboard bear homes? Talk to the salespeople and even a few customers. (If you are going as a large group for a corporate outing, it's a good idea to send an advance crew a day or two before to talk to the store manager and get his/her permission.)

Make sure you spend time talking to each of these groups during your brand safari and that you are looking for "a-ha" moments you can use to TWIST with your brand. Focus on actionable insights. For example, if you were in the Apple store you might observe that the "employees are young and hip." But to take this further to a true "a-ha" moment, you would write down that "employees embody the brand and feel more like users." Then think about how you and your employees could do a better job of embodying your brand and write down a few ideas there in the store, or brainstorm back in the office.

Meet In Locations With A TWIST

Another spin on the brand safari is to hold your next meeting in an unusual, inspirational location. It's amazing how we put people in bland, beige conference rooms and ask them to create ideas that will transform their markets. Why not provide a transformational experience and see what that stimulates?

Recently I led a naming workshop for a global pharmaceutical client. The meeting location was a beautiful ski resort two hours outside of Zurich, Switzerland. Executives had traveled from all over the world to attend this meeting. For the first two days they met in the hotel meeting rooms discussing regulatory issues, timelines and production pathways. Except for the fondue dinner breaks at local restaurants, they could have been anywhere. It was a waste of the majestic alpine scenery and fresh air that Switzerland is famous for. So when it came to the creative part of the meeting, we took 30 executives in a gondola ride to the top of the summit where we did an ice-breaking exercise inside an actual igloo to get the creative juices flowing. Next we had them build and brand their own igloos. And finally we ended up with a creative name brainstorming session in a conference room transformed with floor cushions, mulled wine, cake and local decorations such as cow bells, ceramic milking jars, and even a five-foot red ceramic cow that became the unofficial mascot and muse of the meeting.

Even if you don't have the mountains at your fingertips you can still shake things up and provide a more inspiring environment to work on your brand. You can also turn every day and even the most basic outings into a brand safari – just by observing the world around you and making note of these observations in your brand TWIST journal.

Find TWISTS In Routine Tasks

When my daughter was about ten, an obligatory Girl Scout holiday party turned into a huge source of inspiration for me at Virgin. The first part of the event was all about making gingerbread houses. The girls were consuming more marshmallows and chocolate bars than doing any actual building. They were also partaking from a free-flowing chocolate "lava" fountain. Then something magical happened: the event leader announced it was time for Bingo and asked everyone to take her place. The girls immediately stopped eating, grabbed their Bingo cards, sat down and were silent. This concentration, while a moment before was chaos, was a minor miracle, and it got me thinking about the power of Bingo. It's a game that's been around forever, that people never seem to tire of, and that creates a high degree of focus and anticipation. Everyone wants to be able to shout that magic word "Bingo!"

The next day, I had a meeting with my team to prepare for an upcoming off-site meeting that we were conducting with the marketing leaders of all the individual Virgin companies in North America. The objective of this off-site was to help the different Virgin companies create more cross-company partnerships and ideas that would help loyal Virgin consumers get to know more Virgin brands. Back at work on Monday, I was still thinking about the power of Bingo I witnessed that weekend. Then it hit me. Bingo! We would run this cross-company ideation as a game. We created special Bingo cards with the names of the various Virgin companies across the top and sides. Each time someone came up with an idea that involved the intersection of two of them, they could cover that square. When they had a line of new ideas they could yell "Bingo!" The game was a big success. There was also a level of competition involved, which was very motivating for the Virgin marketing teams. This new technique, which we called Innovation Bingo, was inspired by TWISTING a kids' game with some grown-up objectives at an important meeting.

TWIST Your Down Time

I've written some of my most popular blog posts when on vacation even though I usually try to have a work-free break. But in a relaxed environment, I find I am really able to absorb the nuances of the experiences around me and want to write them down and share them with my followers.

These posts include: "Branding Lessons from the Spa," "Branding Lessons from Summer Camp," and "Branding Lessons from the Ball Park." In each of them, I was open and aware of the brand experience to a degree that I might not have been if I was immersed in my busy workday. I found elements of each unique experience that I could apply to my business and those of my clients and students.

For example, while I haven't been to summer camp in many years, I still enjoy the experience vicariously through my kids' letters home and visiting days. On one such visit a few summers ago, I was so inspired that I wrote an article called "Branding Lessons from Summer Camp" that was published in a major online magazine for women entrepreneurs. The branding lessons from summer camp included: 1) the importance of rituals in brand building – inspired by campfire songs and other camp traditions; 2) the blessing of plans gone astray – inspired by rainy days at camp where scheduled activities are cancelled and you actually have more fun; 3) how competition can actually build team spirit – inspired by the way that dividing a camp into teams for a three-day color war actually brings people together instead of separating them.

Taking breaks and being attuned to experiences and TWISTS while on your downtime can be a useful way to re-energize your mind and body and also to move your business forward.

TWIST Your Colors To Shimmer And Shine

Color and images can be a great source of inspiration; use them to stand out. Remember the sea of sameness of reds and blues mentioned within the banking industry? If I said to you I was thinking of a bank that uses the color orange, would you know which bank I am referring to? Yes, it's ING (now Voya in the U.S.). It has a distinctive and innovative visual identity that really supports its purpose of "Empowering people to stay a step ahead in life and in business." The color orange, which is fresh for the category, underscores the company's fresh approach to helping people understand and leverage their money. It's also a nod to ING's Dutch roots.

When I mention the color robin's egg blue, which brand comes to mind? Tiffany, of course. Its packaging is so distinctive that it creates a lot of anticipation for what unique and beautiful pieces might be inside the box. UPS also delivers packages, but its branding has generally been less iconic until it had an interesting ad campaign by taking a TWIST from Tiffany's and began to celebrate their color with: "What can brown do for you?"

Pay attention to colors that really capture your attention. For example, you might be in the shampoo aisle of your local drugstore and notice a bottle that really stands out. How is that color making you feel? How is it different from other colors around it? Take a few notes in your notebook. Think about the colors that are predominant in your category. How can you TWIST in a different direction and use color as a brand advantage?

Linda transitioned her brand from a traditional family-owned insurance promise to a more modern "We help you Get insurance" brand idea. When she did this, she realized that her red and blue logo developed in the 70s blended in too much with her competitors and undermined her company's TWIST of approachability. She kept the core element of the shape but updated it with vibrant colors, which were inspired by her favorite organic grocer. When she walked into this grocery store, the fruits and vegetables were so inviting and colorful that she wanted to pick them up and put them in her basket. She loved the new logo so much she had it stenciled on the side of her car and created bright throw pillows that adorn the reception area of the agency.

> This splash of color is distinctive for her category and really underscores her brand's intention to be friendlier, more welcoming and more down-to-earth than traditional insurance agencies.

Tips For Activating Your TWISTS

I always encourage my students to try out their new TWISTS on a small scale before making a big announcement or changing over all their materials.

For example:

- Contemplating a new process or pricing policy inspired by your TWIST? Try it in your next client pitch.

- Toying with a new tagline? Try it out in your email signature or as a headline or email subject line. Then do some trademark searches before using it more broadly.

- Developing a new product or service extension? Offer it for free to one of your current clients. Be upfront that you are testing it. They will get value, and you will get input to refine and improve on the idea.

- Have an idea for a book or keynote? Try it out as a blog post. Ask for reactions.

- Working on a product prototype? Make one by hand out of basic materials to make it more real and then share with people who can help move it to the next stage.

- Before you commit to a major website overhaul, create a separate "beta" site consisting of the new look and feel and get reactions.

- Thinking of redoing your logo but not sure what you want? Launch an online 99Designs contest (an online crowd sourced design platform that is often very low cost) to get some ideas of what you want to pursue/ avoid and use this as input for your brand brief to an in-person designer.

- Still working on your brand idea and pillars? Before overhauling your marketing materials start trying it out in conversations and client proposals. Look for the lean-in response.

If you are stuck on any of the above, go search for the TWIST. Think about how a beloved inspirational brand would approach your marketing.

Joanne has a consulting business targeting leaders of non-profits to help them develop stronger organizational and personal development plans. She felt her branding was a bit lackluster and didn't really reflect the passion she felt for her work. She went looking for brands that she felt exuded energy and that she was personally passionate about. She zeroed in on the Mini Cooper, a car she loves to drive because of its unique design, but mostly because she loves the energy she feels when she drives it. She likes feeling close to the road and its iconic design and colors. She TWISTED the Mini with her non-profit brand and created a new website with bold, iconic photographs, splashes of signature orange against black and white images – and a new tagline: "Roadmaps for Successful Social Innovation."

Look At Failure As A Positive TWIST

Failure in branding and in everything you do is inevitable at times. One really important way to learn from failure is to become a student of it. Start to notice in interviews and books when people talk about failure and what it taught them. Think about how you can TWIST those lessons with your brand. One story I love is about Steven Spielberg's making of *Jaws*. I read an interview with him about the making of this movie and how much trouble they were having with the mechanical shark. They couldn't get it to work as well as they wanted and it was supposed to be a very prominent character in many of the scenes. Time and budgets were tight and they couldn't afford to stop shooting and fix the shark every time it malfunctioned. Their adjusted plan was to show less of the actual shark and to show more of the water, while hinting at the shark through a dramatic sound track (dunt, dunt, dah). Spielberg later admitted that this "failure" probably resulted in a more impactful picture. The threat of the shark versus the actual image of it was so much scarier.

Not everyone is able to readily embrace failure. Here's an effective exercise to help you. You are going to purposely create a really bad idea. This idea should be rooted in your business and target, but should be deliberately the opposite of what you would normally do in a market situation. Pick one business challenge to focus this bad idea on. For example, if you want more people to try your new product or service what would be the worst thing you could do?

Here are some questions to guide you in creating this bad idea.

1. What is the opposite of your instinct?

2. What would you do to try and lose money?

3. Who would be the most unlikely target audience?

4. Who shouldn't you partner with?

5. What would go viral in a bad way?

Once you have a really bad idea that would surely get you fired or result in a serious business setback, start to transform it. Highlight one new element that this bad idea exploration led you to and then see if you can find a way to TWIST it into a positive. Build on it until it becomes a plausible idea or direction.

Intermarché, the third largest supermarket chain in France, was concerned about the problem of food waste. They decided to do something about it – with a TWIST. They focused on the "ugly" fruits and vegetables that were normally spurned by customers because they had blemishes or unusual shapes. Instead of hiding these fruits and vegetables at the bottom of the bin, they decided to do something really unexpected: they gave them their own aisle in the store. They launched a poster campaign celebrating the "ugly" produce. At first, customers stayed away from the unwanted cast-offs, but to prove they were just as flavorful as those the customers would normally buy, the store produced soups and juices with the fruits and vegetables for customers to try. The result was a huge success: all stocks of the fruits and vegetables sold out in an initial rush and supermarket traffic overall increased by 24%.

During a Brand School innovation workshop I had executives from an agency that worked with a pharmaceutical client that made a blood clotting medicine complete this exercise. They decided that the worst thing they could do to promote this medicine was to shoot a commercial that was an all-out gore-fest where the blood was flowing out of control. They had a lot of fun imagining the scenario and really loosened up and got into the exercise. When it came time to transform the terrible idea into a plausible one, they realized that a dramatic visualization of the "mechanism of action" of the product was a good idea. Not a blood-fest, but something that had more drama and suspense than they normally showed in the somewhat staid medical demos that were the norm for the category. Sound effects, animation or unusual graphic style or colors would help this demo stand out to jaded medical targets and show how this medicine was dramatically better. This TWIST of "more drama" came directly from the exercise and was something positive they could work with.

Bad Examples Can Also Lead To Great TWISTS

We've mostly talked about positive examples from other brands as a source of inspiration. Another valid way to apply the TWIST is to look at brands that have let you down and think about what you can do differently with your own brand and customers.

I'm an avid tennis fan and was glued to my TV watching Venus and Serena Williams play against each other in the quarter-finals of the U.S. Open. The match that pitted sister versus sister was a big event and had millions of viewers. Not only was it great tennis, but it was a brand sponsoring bonanza with high ratings and close-ups of the players' tennis apparel.

Serena was prominently displaying the Nike logo in several locations on her outfit, but not Venus. She was wearing an original blue and white tennis dress that I really loved, but without a prominently placed and recognizable logo. After some digging on Google, I realized Venus was wearing her own brand called EleVen.

I took note of this misstep and decided to apply this negative TWISTING lesson to my own business. At my next conference presentation, I made sure that there was plenty of Brand School branding around the room so that the women in the audience would know exactly where to go after my talk to get more information to ace their branding.

Lateral thinking and lessons from brands can come in all shapes and sizes. The important thing is to commit to the TWIST as a way of business and life. Actively look for brands that zig while others zag and apply these lessons to your own business.

CHAPTER 7:
YOU ARE YOUR OWN BRAND TWIST

A strong brand is a story well-told and one of the key characteristics of many successful brands is that they leverage the personal TWIST of the founder. It's hard to think of Starbucks without thinking of Howard Schultz, Zappos without Tony Hsieh, Virgin without Richard Branson or *Cosmopolitan* magazine without Helen Gurley Brown. Each of these founders has spent time building their businesses but also paying attention to their own brands and building a reputation for credibility and expertise that helps to support their commercial brand story.

Personal branding is a key element of telling your story and telling it well. You want people to invest in you as an individual, irrespective of what company you work for or what business you are promoting. This is especially important in today's economy when many people have multiple careers over a lifetime or want to look for new opportunities within the same company. It's also critical for entrepreneurs who are often serial entrepreneurs with multiple ideas and ventures over their lifetimes.

Craft And Control Your TWIST

Remember that your personal brand is more of a memoir than an autobiography; make it easy for people to get what you stand for right away.

When sharing details of your personal and professional background, make those details relevant to your target. Too often, I see cleverly written "about me" statements that amuse the reader but don't convince them why they are the right person to do business with. Conversely, traditional bios that include "25 years of experience" in a given field can mean anyone in their mid-40s or 50s. It doesn't set you apart. You need to make that "25 years" mean something to your potential client.

> Cate TWISTED her tenure into a meaningful selling point for her business. She is a professional researcher who worked for large research firms and then eventually went out on her own. She is often hired by clients to run focus groups with consumers to help them get valuable input and feedback on the products and services they are developing. When she felt like her pitches with new clients were falling flat, she decided to add her own TWIST. She re-examined her brand idea and decided to focus her new business efforts on companies and agencies that were operating on "high stakes" projects where they couldn't afford for anything to go wrong. She also repositioned her "25 years' experience" under the benefit of "focused listening" explaining that: "Identifying moments of truth requires focused listening. My philosophy of planning for the best and adapting to the less than ideal enables you to focus your attention on your consumer." This helped her zero in on the clients that were most likely to be interested in a seasoned professional and made her experience more relevant to them.

> She capped off her rebranding by including a personal bio that helped make her passion and experience more tangible: "I was born to moderate. It's like I've been running focus groups since I was little. As the oldest girl in a family of ten, I guided kitchen table conversations, was driven to understand the why behind my siblings' actions and my parents' decisions, and I strove to solve problems. Today, I've built a career on uncovering the why."
>
> Once she started leveraging this TWIST, her new business "hit" rate tripled and she was engaged on several challenging projects that she felt really made the most of her expertise. Her brand story worked because it was inspired, differentiated, rich in detail, and authentic.

Always Be Ready To Share Your TWIST

An important aspect of branding is to make sure you are always ready to seize an opportunity to share your idea with potential stakeholders. These could be funders, partners, future employees, and press. You need to able to communicate quickly and powerfully what your brand stands for and get people excited about your idea in a limited amount of time.

> Erin's dance troupe is dedicated to helping communities that have suffered through traumas such as school shootings or natural disasters, begin the healing process through interactive dance performances and the discussions and community gatherings that often follow. Like many entrepreneurs with

interesting and new ideas, she had trouble articulating what her dance company did. After attending Brand School she created a very simple and elegant brand idea of "Move Together Toward Healing." Afterward, at a charity event, she had the chance opportunity to meet the CEO of an athletic wear company. In a two-minute parking lot conversation she was able to articulate her unique brand TWIST and get him to agree to a follow-up meeting. He was so impressed with her brand that he immediately signed on the dancers in the troupe as spokespeople for his line of innovative dancewear, providing the non-profit with some much-needed capital.

TWIST With People You Admire

A great way to be inspired to tell your own story with a TWIST is to study the stories of people you admire. Note what makes them different and engaging and see how you can apply those storytelling lessons to your own brand.

One famous brand that has influenced my own story is the chef Rachel Ray, even though I have no interest in or real talent for cooking. Despite my lack of culinary skills, I have always admired Rachel Ray. I like how she has set herself apart from the other more serious, and often intimidating, male chefs in her milieu. When she cooks she is very casual, engaging and practical. For example, she might say: "The recipe calls for shallots, but if you have a plain old onion, that's just as good." I like how she calls her cooking magazine *Every Day with Rachel Ray*. I think her TWIST is that she takes cooking off its pedestal and makes it fun, relatable and approachable. Early on, when I was starting my own company, I decided that I wanted to be the "Rachel Ray of Branding" and worked hard to make branding approachable, relatable and fun as well. And from time to time I will watch her TV show or leaf through one of her magazines, not to improve my cooking skills but rather to get inspiration from her brand and TWIST it with my own.

Create A Personal Brand Plan To Develop Your TWIST

Once you know what you stand for, the trick is then to identify a plan to get there. Most business people have professional business plans but you need a personal brand plan as well so you can make sure you are actively building your TWIST. The first step in a personal brand plan is to list your company's brand values and then, for each, take a look at how your personal behavior supports them. For example, are you promoting innovation in your business, but your personal presentation style is quite ordinary? When was the last time you engaged in "innovative" behavior in your personal life such as taking a class in something you know nothing about, going on an out-of-the-ordinary vacation, or learning a new skill relevant to your business? Once you identify these gaps, then you need to write down steps to address them. What one to three things can you do in the next three to six months to be more innovative? Why does this really matter? Because the strongest brands – the ones that stand the test of time through market volatility while creating rabid fans – are the ones that "walk the talk."

Richard Branson is a billionaire in his 60s and a recent grandfather. He could easily slow down but he doesn't. He continues to take on challenges such as climate change, saving the oceans, and setting up programs to help the next generation of entrepreneurs. This is because he fundamentally believes in shaking things up and challenging the status quo. It's not a marketing slogan for him, it's a way of life. And I believe this is a big part of the success of the Virgin brand. Even though Richard is not actually running the day-to-day operations of the 100-plus Virgin businesses around the world, his personal commitment is known, felt and emulated by all of his employees on the front lines. As a result, the brand experience is genuine for customers.

Part of creating an effective personal brand plan is outlining what you want to stand for and picking broad values that transcend any single job position. For example, being known for your business acumen instead of for just being a great accountant. The former allows you more flexibility in your career and could open up more opportunities. Or developing a reputation as a strong creative problem-solver, not just someone who is great at producing a good TV spot. Aiming higher will open up new doors and will help you avoid complacency, which can be an enemy of progress. It is what drives me to constantly TWIST.

Kasha, a young marketing executive, decided to create a personal brand plan to boost her confidence and credibility. She worked with very senior investment advisors and had been at the company almost since finishing university. Kasha wanted to have more impact in her marketing role by being considered more of a thought partner with these colleagues and not just someone who was good at getting pretty brochures and conference materials produced. She outlined where she felt she was in her personal brand, where she wanted to go, and steps she could take to get there. This exercise was not easy for her as she first had to admit there were areas in which she needed help and then commit to closing those gaps. In the end, her personal brand plan paid off. She began to be involved in larger projects and was even flown over from the satellite office in Ireland several times to contribute to important pitches and conferences at the U.S. headquarters. Here's her plan:

From being seen as (Without a TWIST):	To being known as (With a TWIST):	Action Steps
Efficient	Proactive	Build up a network of external contacts that could be useful partners for pitches and thought leadership pieces.
Marketing support	Business partner	Ask to "shadow" a client strategist once a month on an ongoing basis to gain a more in-depth understanding of our business. Ask to attend more client meetings to observe.
Young and eager	Trend expert	Forward trend articles each week with a synopsis of the content and showing a specific link to our business.

It's Never Too Early Or Too Late To Start Building Your Personal Brand TWIST

It's never too early to begin building your personal brand. I speak and teach to middle, high school and college students, and this is something that I stress to all of them. Getting a great job is tough. But in order to increase your chances, you need to get a great education. There are more students than ever applying for the same number of college seats; even schools that were once "safeties" are now tough to get into. Many of the college application essay questions are all about trying to understand your personal brand. The application reviewers are trying to figure out for each student: Can I make sense of you? What is unique about you? What is your TWIST? How will admitting you enrich my institution?

Therefore, it's never too early to identify, build and grow your TWIST whether you are a student or looking for a job. How can you spin your uniqueness into something positive and relevant to your audiences? Sometimes we are so close to our own personal narratives that we don't even see our unique TWISTS, so get input from friends, colleagues, former employers, and professors, anyone who knows you the best.

It is also never too late to build your personal TWIST. Highlighting what is unique about you is important as you consider changing jobs or a career. Here are some questions you can ask colleagues when looking to build your personal brand:

- What do you think is different about working with me than other people in similar roles?

- What were you pleasantly surprised about when working with me?

- What did I bring to the project that you hadn't thought of before?

- If I were to completely change careers, what else could you see me doing?

Sometimes that personal TWIST may not seem relevant to your business strengths, but it is, or can be made to be, if you connect the dots. Remember our trapeze enthusiast who finally embraced that this TWIST was what made her unique as a designer? It took others pointing out that this fundamental aspect of her personal brand could also add a huge TWIST to her business brand.

The TWIST can also be something negative that happened to you but that can be spun into a positive to add depth and empathy to your story.

We can learn a lot from personal failures as well as those in business. Learning to look at setbacks from new angles is one of the most important things you can do to feel more in control of your destiny and soften the impact of these blows.

> Christine had a trifecta of personal setbacks that led to a new, energizing and profitable career. At age 42, three major life events happened in three months. The end of an important romance broke her heart. She almost died when an electrical glitch in her heart proved nearly fatal, despite years of exercise and having just completed a half-marathon the day before. And she walked away from a million-dollar investor causing her business to close. Everything she trusted in was up for grabs but this led to the writing of a best-selling book and the start of a new career as a popular radio host and life coach counseling women entrepreneurs on how to be the curators of their own lives.

We can't always control what happens to us in life, but we can often TWIST these events into new and positive outcomes.

Create A Brand Avatar To Help Hone Your TWIST

While it's very important to develop a strong, authentic personal brand it's also critical for you to remember that there is a difference between you and your personal brand. Your personal brand can be a more empowered version of yourself. In fact, it can be very helpful to create a personal avatar that allows you to do things that you may not feel 100% comfortable or confident doing.

Did you know that Beyoncé, who is a fearless performer, is actually quite shy in real life? Her TWIST to overcome her shyness was to create an alter ego named Sasha Fierce that she would slip into in order to go confidently on stage and entertain millions of fans. Eventually she said goodbye to Sasha Fierce, having built the confidence to self-title her 2013 album *Beyoncé* and to rule the 2013 Super Bowl halftime show with an estimated 111 million viewers. [Sources: *The Washington Post* and ESPN.com]

Maybe your brand avatar can give you more confidence to present in front of groups, to negotiate contracts, or to charge more money for your goods or services. Creating this avatar also helps you decide what elements of your story you want to keep separate and private, and which ones you want to build on.

Really Own Your TWIST

Just as the tone of voice we use with customers plays a big role in establishing our brand to the outside world, the language we use in our own heads and to those closest to us also has a big impact. It's not enough to identify your TWIST, you really need to own it in everything you say and do. It starts with believing in what you stand for and using every interaction – big and small – to demonstrate it. This can mean being more aware of whether you are expressing your TWIST in the conversations you are having as well as in the copy on your website.

> Gail is a life coach who helps guide clients stuck in a cycle of anxiety, stress and depression to finally break free. When working with clients she is a force of positivity, and her TWIST is to help people who have tried everything without success to reach their full potential. However, during our one-on-one sessions in Brand School, she often used the phrase "the problem

is" when referring to the work she was doing in class. Even though she was enjoying the class and making great progress, this negative language was really getting in the way of her reaching her own full potential. Ironically, she would call out this language in her clients but couldn't recognize its negative impact in her own speech. I stressed to her that this was branding, not brain surgery, so she wasn't going to make a "mistake" by going with one tagline over another. It was simply a different path of expression. And starting each of our sessions with "the problem is" was putting both herself and me in a closed frame of mind, the exact opposite of what is required to help build her brand. As soon as she got this, and began TWISTING her own language, she implemented some decisions right away that had a positive impact on her branding and business and her ability to really own her TWIST.

Personal branding is the process by which individuals and entrepreneurs stand out from the crowd. It's your personal TWIST that adds credibility to your business. But it doesn't just develop organically as part of your personality, you need to pay attention to your personal brand. It requires time, attention, and often adjustments and updating. When nurtured properly, it can be a key element in telling an engaging brand story, and a powerful business driver.

CHAPTER 8:
TWISTING IS YOUR MOST IMPORTANT BUSINESS TOOL

Your Brand *IS* Your Business – Repeat After Me

Your brand TWIST cannot be separated from your business. It's ultimately what you are selling. If Starbucks only focused on getting the exact ratio of coffee beans to water right and left the whole experience of drinking coffee as an afterthought, it wouldn't be where it is today. Starbucks would be ignoring its uniqueness and its TWIST. The same is true for your business. No matter what product or service you are offering, your target always has an alternative, whether it's turning to a competitor or doing nothing at all. Your successful business needs a strong TWIST – a compelling reason for consumers to choose and stay loyal to your brand. It's helpful to think of your business and brand as two inextricably linked strands, much like a DNA helix, and to view it as a practical tool that filters every single business decision you make.

Apply Your Brand TWIST To Make Faster, Better Business Decisions

If you are an entrepreneur or small business owner, chances are you have many business ideas that you would like to see come to fruition. If you have too many ideas, and no discipline to stick with one in order to develop it before moving on to the next one, you might have what I call the Magpie syndrome. Magpies are birds that build their nests from a collection of bright, shiny objects. If you are constantly chasing too many ideas at once without seeing your original idea through, you probably have this syndrome, which can be counterproductive and might earn you a reputation as a dreamer not a doer.

A strong brand TWIST can help you avoid this problem while making important decisions faster and with more confidence, plus will help you utilize your limited budget more efficiently.

During the last session of Brand School, we ask students to take one business decision they are grappling with and run it through their brand framework by applying their TWIST to come up with an approach and a plan to get it done.

Here are a few examples of things that students have created:

- New logos and websites that are distinctive and captivating to ideal targets.

- Strategies and specific acquisition tools to build client lists.

- Repackaging of service options to drive increased trial.

- Creation of a brand book to get new partners and vendors on-board.

- Unique and on-brand giveaways and gifts for new clients and referrals.

- Loyalty and retention programs to turn fans into brand ambassadors.

- Blog content strategy and calendar for strong and consistent social media.

- New online courses and live classes/workshops to expand brand reach.

- New pricing reflecting a clearer understanding of value to ideal targets.

- Not-for-profit or charity partnerships that reinforce brand messages.

Your brand TWIST is your unique point of view that should drive behaviors. Great brands don't just bombard us with slogans, they walk the talk of their promise in their actions.

> Bill, a CEO, was tasked with communicating a new look, feel and brand story for his company's financial services firm in a timely and impactful way to its 100 employees, both in the U.S. and Europe. His team originally planned an internal launch similar to what they had done for big announcements in the past: PowerPoint slides and a formal meeting with all the employees. After taking a step back to look at the task of planning this event through the company's brand TWIST, Bill and his team realized the usual strategy was all wrong. Their brand TWIST and what differentiates them in the market is the unique way they create purposeful partnerships with clients as well as how they collaborate as a high-functioning,

ego-less team internally. Through the lens of their brand TWIST, it was suddenly obvious that a "death by PowerPoint" internal brand launch did not reflect their own TWIST objectives. They revamped their approach to include a more locker-room style gathering where Bill and the president told an inspiring story about the firm's journey and what the new name and logo were meant to accomplish. They focused on the fact that while the name and logo were important brand assets, the real assets of the firm were the people who went up and down in the elevators each day.

In the end, there were no distancing PowerPoint slides, just a heartfelt chat that included the chance for employees to provide input and ask questions. The final touch was the whole firm writing their individual signatures on a board that had the new name, logo and tagline printed on it – a ceremony that reinforced that this was a company full of people who lived and breathed the partnership TWIST. There were also cookies and cupcakes with the new logo and balloons with the new colors. All of this added up to a positive, distinctive internal launch that set the new brand off on the right foot.

Evaluate Opportunities For "On" Or "Off" Brand Using Your TWIST

Saying yes to the right on-brand opportunities will lead to more of those opportunities because people tend to travel in tribes of like-minded others. If they are happy with their experience with your brand they will recommend you to others with similar needs.

In order to decide what opportunities are "on-brand" you should create a list of criteria based on your TWIST embodied in your brand idea and brand pillars. Evaluate each new opportunity to see if it has a high, medium or low fit with your brand:

- Does this project play to the strengths of my TWIST?

- Is it something that allows me to connect with and build my ideal target?

- Is it something I feel I am uniquely qualified to deliver on?

- Does it fit with my personal vision and values?

Sometimes, there may be an opportunity that stretches you beyond your brand ideas and pillars. In that case, ask yourself:

- Will this give me a new experience that I don't currently have?

- Will this introduce me to valuable contacts or open new doors?

- Will it take me to a new geography or introduce me to new people?

- Is it financially significant enough (although not directly on brand) that it will help me fund other "on brand" activities?

Don't take on a project for its financial potential alone if it does not meet any of the previous criteria or could potentially be brand damaging and confuse people about what your brand stands for.

Use Your TWIST To Say No

Part of being a successful entrepreneur is knowing when to say no, using your brand idea and pillars as your filter and guide. Remember your brand idea is your overarching brand promise and your pillars are the brand values that support this idea. Prioritize actions and opportunities that build a cohesive brand story and let the other things go. There will be many interesting ideas and opportunities that cross your path but before pursuing them, take out your brand framework and use your TWISTS as an evaluation tool. How does this opportunity help me strengthen or more effectively or efficiently deliver my brand idea? Does it deliver on at least two of my three brand pillars? If it doesn't, then either go back and rework it until it does or let it go.

Here are some examples of "no" decisions that were made by Brand School students:

- Saying no to taking on a new client that did not value their TWIST.

- Saying no to expanding into new products that, while lucrative, would distract from their story and a clear communication of their TWIST.

- Saying no to licensing their product where they would no longer have control of their TWIST.

- Saying no to expanding their target to a new segment that was easy pickings but not strategic and did not really appreciate their TWIST.

- Saying no to discounting their services, which was buoyed by new clarity on the true value of their TWIST.

Remember This Framework To Develop Your TWIST

You may think since branding seems like a creative exercise that it should be an organic process with no framework. However, creativity needs constraints and a framework to thrive.

A non-structured approach and a pure blank sheet of paper is actually the hardest way to ideate. Where do you begin? How do you know the idea is rooted in any tangible need? Ask anyone who is creative for a living (writers, fine artists, graphic designers, structural designers) and they will tell you that the parameters put on a project help, not hinder, their creativity. For example, many writing courses will give you a "prompt" to begin an assignment. This can be a sentence, a photograph, an object – something to spark an idea – and where it goes after that is up to you.

Branding is not brainstorming. Coming up with the ideas is the easy part. It's figuring out what to do with these ideas and bringing them to market where most people struggle. An idea is useless without a plan to develop it and get it out into the world.

As a reminder, a branding framework helps you think through the four key questions that any strong brand must ask and identifies the role of the TWIST in creating a compelling, distinctive answer.

1. WHO? are the most profitable targets for the brand?

TWIST to zero in on specific emotional triggers

2. WHAT? will compel them to choose you and stay loyal?

TWIST to create a more distinctive brand promise

3. WHY? should these high-priority targets believe?

Add your personal TWIST for a stronger story

4. HOW? is the brand felt in every touch point?

TWIST with brands you admire for fresh ideas

Each of these questions needs time, energy, and an exploration of your TWISTS to help your brand stand out. They should be answered in order, and they should be viewed as interdependent on one another.

Here's a recap of the importance of each, now that you have seen the many benefits of answering each of these questions with your own unique TWIST.

The "who" is your ideal target. Having a specific, narrow and well-defined target is the most important thing you can do for your brand. It allows you to create a powerful "what" that is your unique and compelling brand idea – or brand promise. A strong brand promise should help you connect with your targets' hearts, not just their heads. It is supported by the "why" – your three brand pillars. If the "what" is the roof of your brand's house, the "why" are the critical support beams. Why should customers and partners believe that you can deliver on your brand promise? What is your unique background, point of view on the category, and approach to delivering your goods or services? Lastly, even the best brand strategy is useless if we don't experience it in the real world and off the paper. This is where the "how" comes in. How are the brand idea and pillars brought to life in every transaction and at every touch point like your website, tone of voice, packaging, social media, and personal brand?

Top Ten Takeaways For Successful TWISTING

Remember these key takeaways that we have covered throughout the book. If you have questions about any of these, go back and review the chapters listed.

1. A great brand is a story well-told (chapter 1).

2. Open your eyes, remove your brand blinders (chapter 2).

3. Define your brand first, then market (chapter 3).

4. Speak to people's hearts – not just their heads (chapter 3).

5. Everyone is not your target (chapter 4).

6. Look for under-utilized moments of magic (chapter 5).

7. Train your brain to think differently (chapter 6).

8. Use words, colors, and images to stand out (chapter 6).

9. You are your brand (chapter 7).

10. Branding is a key business tool (chapter 8).

A TWIST That Endures

When I think back to that McDonald's Airlines moment over ten years ago, the lesson I learned that day is just as valid today as it was then. The rise of the smartphone and the "third screen" of media means that we are bombarded by even more messages and it's becoming harder and harder to stand out. Creating and expressing your unique and compelling point of view in your market with your TWIST is critical, particularly for small business owners, non-profits, and solopreneurs, and even for big companies.

I've seen first-hand the power of the TWIST transform hundreds of students and businesses, and I still get the same thrill as I did that day in the airport. I love the passion that rises to the surface when they uncover their TWIST and fall in love, or sometimes back in love, with their businesses. I consider it a privilege to help people along this journey toward clarity, differentiation, and impact. I will forever be grateful for that McDonald's mirage that helped me understand my own TWIST and led me to help so many others pursue theirs.

Share The Story Of Your TWIST

We'd love to hear about your journey to uncover your TWIST whether you are just beginning your business, struggling to uncover your story or have a success you want to share. Join us at www.TheTwistBook.com to continue the conversation and connect with a community of dynamic small business owners and entrepreneurs.

If you would like more information on the Brand School case studies included in this book, feel free to reach out to me at Julie@BrandTwist.com. And if you feel like the time is right for more support, please visit us at www.BrandSchoolonline.com and fill out an application for a Brand Health Check. This is a 45-minute strategy session where we will offer advice on your specific branding challenges and help you begin your own journey to defining, strengthening, and expressing your TWIST.

ABOUT THE AUTHOR

Photo credit: Bob Plotkin

Julie Cottineau is the creator of Brand School by BrandTwist, a unique and actionable online branding class for entrepreneurs, small businesses and non-profits. Her unique TWISTING approach helps businesses remove their brand blinders and look outside of their categories for actionable insights that are applied to build stronger brands that stand out and deliver better business results.

Before starting her own brand school and consultancy, Julie honed her branding chops at a series of high-level agency positions including as vice president management supervisor at Grey Global in both the U.S. and France and executive director of consumer branding at Interbrand. She has client-side experience as the vice president of brand at Richard

Branson's Virgin Management Group overseeing branding strategy for new and established Virgin companies in North America.

Julie loves to teach and talk about branding and has been an adjunct professor and visiting senior lecturer at Columbia and Cornell Universities as well as a frequent branding commentator on Twitter at @jcottin and in top business media such as Forbes.com, *Entrepreneur Magazine*, CNN, and American Express Open Forum.

Her own life has been full of magical TWISTS that have brought her to reside in Westchester County, NY, with her French husband and two wonderful children. Oh, and she is the unofficial inventor of the Pet Rock.

Notes:

Notes:

Notes: